MW00425350

Introduction by Patricia T. Holland

# Choosing Motherhood

Stories of Successful Women Who Put Family First

Compiled by Lia Collings
Edited by Elise Hahl and Rosalyn Eves

CFI
An Imprint of Cedar Fort, Inc.
Springville, Utah

ISBN 13: 978-1-4621-1183-1

Published by CFI, an imprint of Cedar Fort, Inc., 2373 W. 700 S., Springville, UT 84663
Distributed by Cedar Fort, Inc. www.cedarfort.com

LIBRARY OF CONGRESS CATALOGING-IN-PUBLICATION DATA

Choosing motherhood : stories of successful women who put family first / compiled by Lia Collings ; edited by Elise Hahl and Rosalyn Eves ; introduction by Patricia T. Holland.
pages cm
ISBN 978-1-4621-1183-1
1. Motherhood--Religious aspects--Church of Jesus Christ of Latter-day Saints. 2. Church of Jesus Christ of Latter-day Saints--Doctrines. I. Collings, Lia, editor of compilation. II. Hahl, Elise, editor. III. Eves, Rosalyn, editor. IV. Holland, Patricia T., 1942- author of introduction, etc.
BX8643.W66C49 2013
248.8'4310882893--dc23

2012048491

Cover design by Rebecca J. Greenwood
Cover design © 2013 Lyle Mortimer
Edited by Emily S. Chambers
Typeset by Alyssa Hodge

Printed in the United States of America

10 9 8 7 6 5 4 3 2 1

Printed on acid-free paper

# CONTENTS

CONTENTS

# PREFACE

In an August 2009 address to seminary and institute teachers, Sister Julie B. Beck encouraged instructors to teach their students "the doctrine of the family." The essays that follow comprise the testimonies of sixteen women concerning that doctrine, specifically the doctrine of motherhood. For some, this testimony came easily and early on. For others, it required study, prayer, and much faith. For a few, it came after many tears. For all, these testimonies were grounded in the fundamental truths that we are children of God and that the Lord loves His children. Though we, like Nephi, do not know the meaning of all things, we have learned by experience that we can trust Him to direct us for good if we counsel with Him in all our doings. We offer these experiences as our evidence.

# INTRODUCTION

My first thought regarding this delightfully moving collection of essays was that I am old enough to be the mother—and with only a little stretch, the grandmother!—of the remarkable women who wrote them. (Interesting that I would instinctively "choose motherhood" to measure my relationship to more than a dozen women I have never met.) That was my first thought, and, truth to tell, it made me feel a bit ancient. But my second thought rushed in and carried the day; I was boldly, determinedly, fearlessly young again, a relatively newly married twenty-something packing up our U-Haul, casting both caution and good sense to the wind and turning my face, two children's diaper bags, and my husband's academic hopes toward New Haven, Connecticut. With each of these remarkably articulate stories I laughed and cried and remembered. How I wish this book had been written when Jeff and I were dreaming the dreams of youth—with twenty-eight-hour days, more month than money, and, as one of the authors writes, "children on every square inch of my body."

As the preface indicates, these testimonies—because that

is what they are—come from sixteen young mothers who studied, or supported their husbands who studied, at Yale University. That is why they invited me to write this introduction, linking their lives in New England in the twenty-first century with mine back before the Battles of Concord and Lexington. But these are not stories about Yale. They have nothing to do with the Ivy League or silver academic spoons in anyone's mouth or upscale professions. They are not even stories about education—at least not traditional classroom education. They are, rather, stories about young lives, high hopes, choices to make, and gowns—maternity, not academic, hospital, or judicial—with the undeniable evidence of a baby's digestive system embedded permanently near the neckline. They are stories about prayers and priorities, about dreams pursued and dreams deferred, about five- and ten- and twenty-year plans being replaced by recurring twenty-four-hour cycles of chaos. They are stories about babies who wouldn't stop crying and mothers who couldn't. They are stories about anxiety that one has conceived and greater anxiety that one hasn't. They are stories about a baby's smile "making it Christmas every day," about this being "the good life—the only one I want," about "teaching souls to fly." Above all, they are stories about the faith and miracle of maternal love.

I began by saying I was older now. What I really want that to mean is that I think I am a little wiser now, that I think I see things a little more clearly now, that I have walked a little farther on the road young mothers in this Church are now walking. And my call to the tens of thousands of those just starting that road is that nothing in my life—nor anything I can imagine in the next life—compares with the joy I have felt as a mother. I too chose motherhood. And it is a tragedy (I use the word in its classic sense) that in some circles in our day, it may become, as one New Englander phrased it, "the road less traveled by." But for those who do choose it, motherhood will in time and in eternity "make all the difference."

*Patricia T. Holland*

# GRADUATION

*by Jennifer Frahm*

Breathe. Relax. Concentrate. Repeat. The sun was breaking on the horizon. Somehow, the entire night had passed. This observation drifted into my mind in the ten seconds between sets of double contractions. Now I was gripping my husband's hand, listening for my doula's voice, and surrendering again to the intensity. Everything else faded into oblivion. After what might have been lifetimes, I found myself lying down, dressed in a hospital gown, surrounded by a doctor and several nurses in hospital uniform. As I looked up, I also saw my husband extending a bundle toward me. I looked into the face of a peaceful, perfect little creature. He peered into my eyes intently, as if searching my soul. Joy and disbelieving gratitude welled up in my heart. In an instant, my life changed forever. But it would require further reflection to see how an earlier, similarly momentous experience played a key role in my being in the hospital that morning.

Four years earlier, I had been in a similar state of excitement and anticipation, awaiting a climactic event as I sat next to some of my best friends, wearing identical black caps and gowns. When my name was called, I proudly walked to the podium, shook hands with officials dressed in their royal-colored robes, and gingerly gripped my diploma. After sitting, I eagerly examined the indecipherable Latin until my finger came to rest on my name—the only familiar text in the document. Relief, satisfaction, and a sense of great accomplishment welled up within me. Even though I knew the diploma I held was just a pretty piece of paper, what it represented was far greater—not just the courses and exams I'd completed at Yale, but also the experiences I'd had, the people I'd met, and the ways I'd changed.

Alchemists of the late fifteenth century coined a term for this momentous event, a term that only several centuries later became associated with the conferral of an academic degree: *graduation*. Originally, *graduation* meant "tempering, refining of something to a certain degree." Graduation was an important principle for alchemists, who sought to capture the art of converting otherwise undesirable or even harmful metals like lead into gold or silver by applying chemicals or heat. The modern concept of academic graduation retains remnants of this ancient meaning. Through a series of courses and exams, we refine our understanding of a particular body of knowledge, until we reach a certain degree of mastery. Today, however, graduation has become associated less with this process than with the event that marks its completion.

Reflecting on my years at Yale, though, I realize that not only was I working toward a one-time graduation *event*, but that there was indeed a more subtle graduating *process* occurring at the same time. This process—this *other* graduation—was not directly related to my academic studies, nor did it have an academic outcome, although it was linked to, and in many ways dependent on, my academic environment. Simply put, the process that took place during my university years consisted of learning to sacrifice good things for better things. Sacrifice is a key element in graduation because it is most often sacrifice that initiates the process of graduation—that is, the process of tempering and refining—in the first place. Let me share a few instances of sacrifice from my life that contributed to my *other* graduation.

Perhaps it goes without saying that the people and ideas at Yale challenged my beliefs on all fronts. This was, after all, what I had anticipated and hoped would happen. The challenges did not always come in the expected forms, however. As a senior, I was selected to the position of freshman counselor. FroCos not only live among freshmen, receiving free board, but are also expected to counsel freshmen on academic, social, and personal issues. Freshman counselor is a very public position. It confers definite status. FroCos are, in a word, cool. I was cool. That is, until my fellow FroCo and good friend, Kim, pulled me into her room one late October day and dropped a heavy question: "Are you sure you're allowed to date Walker?" Walker was an LDS freshman I had been dating for about three weeks. He was not in my counseling group, or even in my residential college. Rereading the terms of my contract, however, my mistake became clear. All freshmen were off limits.

Stunned, I spent several hours pondering my predicament. This wasn't a long-standing relationship, nor was it likely to become serious in the near future: Walker and I were each planning on serving a mission after the academic year ended, and besides, we were still so young. From almost any perspective, it would be foolishness to give up my position to pursue a relationship that was so apparently insubstantial. But prayers confirmed my true feelings: this relationship was one I should not abbreviate. My only hope was that if I could explain LDS dating standards to the administration, they would realize this relationship was not inappropriate. My branch president consented to take over this task. After he spoke with my dean, I entered her office, sat down uncomfortably in a stiff chair, and faced her. A few exotic trinkets adorned the desk, but no plants, paintings, or personal paraphernalia welcomed me. I began awkwardly explaining that I hadn't understood the rules, and that nothing in our relationship was inappropriate. Her face remained expressionless. Before I could even announce that I wasn't going to stop dating Walker, she stated, with a look of barely concealed indifference, "You're fired."

Tears stung my eyes. All of two minutes had elapsed, but I had nothing else to say. I made my way outside into the warm sunshine of a November day, oblivious to anything but my own spinning world. Though I understood my dean's position, I was indignant. My beliefs about dating and my adherence to high standards of moral conduct had been completely discounted, to say nothing of my honesty in bringing this situation to the attention of the administration. A few hours after being fired, and after a very emotional conversation with Walker, however, the unexpected feeling that settled within me was peace.

Still, it was embarrassing to explain this situation to my freshmen. It was humiliating to move across campus, back to my residential college home, and face dozens of well-intentioned questions. How could I explain my choice without resorting to the hashed "true love" excuse? The truth was, I didn't know if our relationship would continue much longer, but the Lord had told me that I needed to maintain this relationship, perhaps because it had the potential to become eternal. I had chosen to sacrifice something good—my position—for the possibility of something far better—an important relationship. This was a turning point in my thinking about what I would sacrifice to maintain important relationships, and it was a critical step in helping me choose motherhood later on. Making this choice has made me more willing to choose difficult things, and to accept difficult consequences for doing the right thing. This sacrifice tempered me—it made me stronger and more resilient—and earned me a course credit toward my *other* graduation, the one that marked my improved ability to make good sacrifices.

A second experience that taught me about sacrifice happened after I finished my BA in May 2005. I had decided to serve a full-time mission after graduation. But I had also elected to do a year of MA coursework while working on my BA, which meant that I would still have one year of graduate coursework to complete after I returned from my mission. Leaving mid-program like this also meant that I would have to reapply to the MA program and might not be readmitted. Nevertheless, I chose a mission. Toward the end of my eighteen months, I submitted two documents required for reapplication: one new academic recommendation, and a new admissions essay. Six weeks later, a rare piece of mail arrived from the university. Sitting at a kitchen table in Jönköping,

Sweden, and weary after a long missionary day, I opened the letter. Seconds later, stunned and confused, I reread the single paragraph. Denied admission? I knew people on the admissions committee. One of my advisers, a senior faculty member, had told me before I left that my readmission was virtually assured. I'd already done a full year of coursework! The next day, I got permission from my mission president to call Graduate Admissions to double-check that all of my application materials had been received. The officer who took my call checked his files and resumed our conversation: "I'm at a total loss." A secretary had neglected to attach my previous application materials, which included three recommendations and test scores. As a result, the only materials presented to the admissions committee had been the new recommendation and essay. I called my former adviser. He promised to look into the issue. But I knew the chances of being admitted at so late a date were slim. Decisions had been mailed and financial offers made.

Unexpectedly, while making these phone calls, a feeling of total trust and reassurance replaced my anxiety. Just as before, the feeling that settled within me was peace. This feeling never changed or left, even after I arrived home from my mission and waited several more weeks for any news. Finally, an admissions director called. They were very sorry for the mistake, he explained. My adviser had insisted that they reconsider my application, which they had. Though they had already admitted the maximum number of students for that year, they made some adjustments. Amazingly, I was offered readmission. My surprise grew to astonishment when, a few days later, I was extended a full-tuition fellowship and stipend. My gratitude to God was boundless. I knew when I chose a mission that I was also choosing the possibility I wouldn't be readmitted to graduate study. But after receiving the rejection letter, I also realized that, if I were denied readmission, I had sacrificed something good—a year of graduate coursework—for something that was far better—service as a missionary. In this case, the Lord didn't require an actual sacrifice, but only my willingness to make it. This experience tested my trust in the Lord, but it ultimately fortified my faith in the promise of sacrifice—that it will be repaid with even greater bounty. This experience became another course credit toward my *other* graduation.

In May of 2008, I finished my MA in European and Russian studies but missed commencement so that I could marry Walker. I wasn't waiting one more day. During the following summer, I worked as a research assistant for one of my professors, known for her intellectual prowess as much as for her kindness. I loved visiting her corner office, chock-full of books and cluttered with boxes. Everything about her environment and her personality was relaxing. And our conversations were as much about my future as they were about her research.

"The papers you wrote for my course were really creative. You could definitely work on some of your ideas and get published . . . have you considered a PhD? I think you would make a great candidate in my department."

The praise felt good, really good. "You think so? Yes, I've thought about a PhD. I'm just not sure I'm ready to commit to six more years of school. I also want to have kids, and I'm not sure I could do both at the same time."

My professor had in fact done her PhD while raising a child. She had only positive things to say: "Doing a PhD with a child was great. In fact, I can't think of another occupation that would have been as flexible for me while raising a child."

I really wanted to believe this could be true for me. Perhaps it could have been true. But, at that time, I simply didn't feel impressed that I should go on for a PhD. Instead of feeling distressed or concerned about my future, though, I felt at peace. About six months after this conversation, my husband and I felt the time was right to start having children. I was instantly filled with reassurance, knowing that the Lord had a plan for my life, and that he had guided me onto a particular path.

Looking back, I realize that my decision to postpone a PhD was inspired. My laughing, curious, strong-willed little boy demands a good deal of my energy, and I want to be able to give it to him. Knowing myself, I don't think I would feel satisfied being able to devote only the small remainder of my energy to academic studies. Perhaps in another stage of life the balance will shift. This sacrifice was one of faith—I did not know beforehand that the academic opportunity I was giving up would be replaced by something more valuable. In fact, I am still exercising faith that this is true. This experience was another course credit earned toward my *other* graduation, because I learned that I could make major sacrifices even when I'm not sure of the outcome.

But, having chosen to postpone a PhD and pursue motherhood full time, other goals and experiences outside of motherhood are still necessary for me to feel fulfilled. Elder M. Russell Ballard has taught:

> Even as you try to cut out the extra commitments, sisters, find some time for yourself to cultivate your gifts and interests. Pick one or two things that you would like to learn or do that will enrich your life, and make time for them. Water cannot be drawn from an empty well, and if you are not setting aside a little time for what replenishes you, you will have less and less to give to others, even to your children. . . . Don't allow yourself to be caught up in the time-wasting, mind-numbing things . . . Turn to the Lord in faith, and you will know what to do and how to do it.[1]

I love running, listening to podcasts, composing music, discussing difficult questions, making food for my family and friends, tutoring students, taking classes, writing, and spending time by myself. Could I dispose of all of these loves of mine and still be fulfilled? No. In fact, if I did, I would have much less energy and enthusiasm to serve my family. That said, even without children, no way could I fully pursue *all* of these interests. As a mother, I have learned that it is indeed important to pursue my own interests, but only in a deliberate fashion—and only after I've carefully weighed my needs, the needs of my family, and the needs of those around me, and then chosen the most meaningful pursuits for my particular stage of life.

Choosing deliberately how to spend my time is critical for me to feel fulfilled. I recall a conversation I had with a close LDS friend about our future lives. My friend explained that her mother was an outspoken proponent of careers for every Mormon woman. Her mother had perhaps met too many women who were unhappy, depressed, or unfulfilled in their roles as mothers, and she believed the solution was a career. However, after carefully considering my friend's mother's viewpoint, I have discovered my own personal antidote to this concern: *choice*. I have concluded that I cannot be satisfied in my motherly role unless I actively choose, embrace, and love that role. The scriptures teach plainly that there are "things to act and things to be acted upon" (2 Nephi 2:14). They also teach that the ability to choose requires at least two available options. In some cases, there are only two options—good and evil. In other cases, there are two or three or more options that vary in their degree of desirability. In no case, however, are we truly making a choice when there is only one option. It follows that we also cannot make a true sacrifice when there is only one option. If a needy individual steals two hundred dollars from me, this is considered a misfortune or trial; but if I *choose* to give this money to the same needy individual, it is considered a sacrifice. Even though in both cases, I lose two hundred dollars and a needy person gains two hundred dollars, the spiritual outcomes are not the same for either of us. Perhaps the best illustration of choice as a necessary element in sacrifice can be found in the atonement of Jesus Christ. In order for Christ's infinite sacrifice to be effectual, He had to choose it.

Following this line of reasoning, I have recognized that, in order for me to find fulfillment as a mother, I must always *choose* motherhood. This means that I must also have other viable options, including pursuing another academic degree, a career, or other professional role. I never want to feel forced into full-time mothering or feel I've simply fallen into this role—not just for my own well-being, but also for the well-being of my children. I want them to clearly see and understand that I have *chosen* full-time mothering and *chosen* them. Having chosen to mother my children full-time instead of other full-time occupations—that is, having sacrificed for motherhood—I find greater meaning and increased satisfaction in this vital role.

The small sacrifices I have made—to give up being a cool FroCo, to be willing to sacrifice readmission to an MA program, and to postpone a PhD—have helped me earn course credits toward my *other* graduation. What is this *other* graduation? It is a process that has improved my ability to sacrifice good things for better things. Just as we are imperfect masters of our chosen disciplines when we graduate from college, I am still a very imperfect master of the principle of sacrifice. But I have become better at it. I have graduated one step further.

Why do these experiences continue to matter so much to me? First, because I believe the Lord used these experiences to prepare me for the sacrifice of motherhood—the constant sacrifice of time, energy, and resources to serve children. Second, because what really happened was not an event but a *process*. Many memorable events take place in my life as a mother, but far more of my time and energy is devoted to day-to-day tasks, responsibilities, and activities. Taken together, these small actions are the elemental building blocks of life that represent the process of becoming. Over time, just like the alchemist converting metal into gold, these small actions—many of them small sacrifices—will temper and refine us, converting us into priceless gems.

Giving up much of my time and independence to care for an infant; expending all of my energy to meet the needs of a curious toddler; exercising all of my patience to teach children to share, respect, love, and forgive; mustering all of my courage to communicate with teenagers; searching myself for enough faith to meet the spiritual needs of a developing soul—all of these opportunities to sacrifice in the service of my children *graduate* me. They refine me. They temper me. Through an eternal process, a wise and merciful Father in Heaven teaches me truths, and I master these truths one degree at a time. As a mother, I believe I will take part in more of these kinds of "graduations" than in any other role.

When I received my degrees, dressed in academic regalia, I celebrated an academic graduation. When I became a mother, dressed in a hospital gown, I was celebrating a spiritual graduation. Ultimately, I hope to take part in a final graduation, or rather, commencement: the end of mortal life and the beginning of life eternal, when the Lord will clothe His faithful followers in the robes of righteousness.

# "YOU WILL BE A SUCCESSFUL MOTHER"

*by Sarah Clayton*

It was 3:00 a.m., and I was just leaving the office. I had logged twenty hours that day and was bleary-eyed, hungry, and, well, truth be told, I didn't mind one bit. Satisfied at last with the briefing paper I had been meticulously crafting all day, I pushed "send," triple-checking to make sure it went successfully. It would be printed and copied, bound with a minute-by-minute itinerary, and placed on Mrs. Bush's desk before she woke in a few short hours.

I turned off the computer, grabbed my purse, and peered out my window overlooking the South Lawn to my left and the Executive Residence to my right. The third floor where the First Family slept was still and dark, but the offices of the West Wing were lit as usual. I wondered what occupied them tonight. A high-stakes military maneuver? A visit from a head of state? Perhaps an early morning vote on Capitol Hill. I dimmed the lights and started down the hall of the East Wing, past the social secretary's desk, the calligraphers' studio, and, finally, the Chief of Staff's office. Along the walls hung giant photographs of Mrs. Bush on her most recent trip to Africa.

I exited into the sticky morning air, scanning my badge, pushing through the turnstile, and raising my hand as if to say "good night" to the Secret Service agent inside his glass booth. Fireflies flittered around the lampposts that lit the way down East Executive Avenue. I couldn't help but think of the many people that had walked this walk before me—heads of state, Cabinet officials, decorated war heroes, Nobel laureates, and many ordinary people that had managed to do not-so-ordinary things. As was my habit, I closed the gate behind me and then looked over my shoulder. I felt the need to remind myself that the gate wasn't a separation between my dreams and my reality but the actual entrance to 1600 Pennsylvania Avenue, the place where *I* worked.

Six o'clock was departure time. I was back at the White House in my finest suit and shiniest pair of patent leather heels, hugging my binder and pacing the length of the Diplomatic Reception Room. At a quarter till seven, the stretch limo pulled into the roundabout that formed a black "u" on the South Lawn. Like clockwork, the processional ensued—first her Chief of Staff, then her press secretary, followed by her personal assistant, photographer, and transcriptionist. Then FLOTUS (White House speak for "First Lady of the United States") herself climbed into the limo ahead, her Secret Service agent, "Big Bird," fast behind her.

The drive to Andrew's Air Force Base was quick—for motorcades, it always was. We boarded Bright Star, and I searched for my seat card, embossed with the Presidential seal and calligraphed with my name. FLOTUS sat quietly in the front of the plane studying the very briefing paper I had finished just hours before. Before long, we landed in Mobile,

Alabama, where she visited a summer camp for fatherless boys. Gracious as always, she was anxious to hear what the boys were learning in school. She listened to them sing a song prepared for her, and even joined them in a three-legged race. She smiled, waved, shook hands, and posed before being whisked away. Moved by the boys' stories, she glowed about the event the whole way back, anxious to continue her work on behalf of underprivileged youth.

Back at the White House, I gathered my things and hailed a cab at the corner of Pennsylvania and 15th Street. Thrilled with another successful event, I took in the Washington, DC, skyline from the freeway. I cracked my window to let in the summer breeze and contemplated my future, convinced that this city, which had enchanted me for so long, held even greater things in store.

* * * * * * *

But the Lord had different plans. Another season of life—marriage and motherhood—was just around the corner. In fact, I had unknowingly met my future husband just a few weeks before. As our relationship progressed, I contemplated what it would require for me to take the first step away from the city—and the work—that I loved. I had made an eight-year investment in my professional path and had charted my course to the White House. Would I be able to walk away?

Call me crazy, but I liked working. I liked laboring over those late-night briefing papers, sifting through hundreds of emails each day, flying across the country at all hours of the day and night, and spending way too much time perfecting that one

PowerPoint slide. Whether it was the White House or somewhere else, I thrived in environments where I was advocating for the causes I cared about, where the goals were clear, my performance was measurable, and the rewards were regular.

With marriage and motherhood, much about my life would change. I would trade cross-country flights on the First Lady's plane for weekly trips to Safeway. Instead of stimulating discussions with colleagues on current events, the topic of the day would be what my child did—or, more likely, didn't—eat for dinner. It would mean good-bye to the steady stream of perks—fireworks on the Fourth of July from the South Lawn, Marine One takeoffs, and invitations to White House Christmas parties. Instead, I would be lucky to get a "thank you, Mom." A homebound lifestyle, less time with colleagues and friends, many repetitive responsibilities, longer hours, few-and-far-between rewards . . . did I want to sign up for this?

But in the end, I was concerned about something more fundamental than just enjoying motherhood. I was worried that I didn't have what it takes. At age twenty-seven, I had invested far more in developing the skills to be successful in the workplace than in those required to be successful in the home. A "career" in motherhood felt almost as foreign to me as a career in professional wrestling.

In my grandmother's era, women were schooled in child rearing and all the trappings of domestic life. The pressure to master the activities of the home front came not only from Latter-day Saint culture but also from a larger society that still held to traditional notions of a woman's responsibilities. Growing up in the 1980s and 1990s, the message I internalized was that all opportunities were available to me, and, as a result, I developed what seemed to be my natural skill set, preparing for a career outside the home. Not only that, but my personal circumstances were such that I had little interaction with children. I had no young siblings to care for, I didn't babysit as a teenager, and geography separated me from my siblings' children. Oh, and I was a lousy cook.

No reasonable person comparing my credentials against any job description of motherhood would have hired me. More than a testimony of motherhood, what I needed was a testimony of *me* as a mother.

Later that summer, the Lord drew me to the pages of my patriarchal blessing, where I found words that, I have no doubt, were written for my twenty-seven-year-old self to read on that very day. There, He told me that my children would love one another. They would love their parents. The household I would create with my husband would be a refuge against the world. Then came the words that meant the most: "You will be a successful mother." It was as if I were reading them for the first time.

That was enough for me to take the first step. In December of that year, my husband, Will, and I were married. Less than two years later, in September 2009, I became a mother for the first time, giving birth to a precious baby boy.

At this writing, Liam is nearly a year old. If you were to ask me to bear my testimony of motherhood today, I could easily do so. It is, not surprisingly, stronger than it has ever been. If you asked me to bear my testimony of myself as a mother, I might hesitate, but only because it is a work in progress, a continuous chain of small impressions, manifestation and experiences that, when linked together, are building something stronger and more sure. Below I share a few of the links in that chain—powerful experiences with motherhood—that have taught me abundantly in just twelve short months, my four seasons of motherhood.

## *September 23*

My husband, Will, had just left for post-MBA job interviews when Liam, then just two weeks old, began crying inconsolably. After several long hours of bouncing, burping, pacing, and back patting, my patience waned and my worry grew. At a complete loss—and affected by some powerful postpartum hormones—I too became inconsolable and joined my son in a duet of fear and frustration. I was exhausted and alone, and for the first time in my life, another's life was entirely in my hands.

The crying continued into the early morning hours, and it occurred to me that I should take Liam to the emergency room, but I fought the idea. His temperature wasn't high enough. It would be an expensive visit. Plus, the idea of packing the diaper bag, getting Liam into the car seat in the dark night, and driving to the hospital on so little sleep completely overwhelmed me.

I began to panic. My many fears about not being up to the task of motherhood found their way to the surface. Was there nothing I could do to make it better? Again, the impression came to go to the emergency room. Reluctantly, we went. After a long wait and several rounds of tests, the doctor declared Liam to be just fine. Other than a slight temperature, he was perfectly healthy.

I felt foolish. Why the impression? Why the difficult late-night trip? It all seemed like wasted effort. Only in retrospect do I understand. We did not go to the hospital that night for Liam. We went for me. It was a loving Heavenly Father's way of pulling a tired, overwhelmed mother out of a dark place and into a public place with caring people who could give me the help and peace of mind I needed. It was as simple as that. **Lesson learned:** *No one could possibly be up to the task of raising children on their own, but the Lord is our partner, and He is always up to it.*

## December 20

It was hours before the neighborhood Christmas nativity pageant. Liam had been cast as a sheep and still didn't have a costume. I didn't sew, my experiment with cotton balls and a glue gun was an utter failure, and it was too late to order something online. Deflated, I threw a brown, woolly blanket over his coat and called it good.

When we arrived at the pageant, feelings of inadequacy immediately crept over me. Forget about a neighborhood nativity pageant . . . this felt more like an evening on Broadway. We were standing in a backyard filled with wise men, shepherds, and angels whose mothers had, it seemed, spent weeks hand crafting the most elaborate costumes I could imagine. It would never have even occurred to me to invest so much time and effort. Embarrassed by my paltry attempt at a costume, I pulled Liam from the lineup, took the blanket off, and held him in the back while the other children acted out the Christmas story. Maybe no one would notice us.

Liam couldn't yet speak, but on the way home, I could hear his voice in my head. "I was the only kid at the pageant without a costume. My mom doesn't sew. She's not creative. She doesn't do this or that." So little of what I had learned in graduate school or the workforce was of any use in my new role. There was so much I didn't know and so much I didn't know how to do.

As I shared the experience with a close friend, she said, "If you're worried that Liam won't ever have the most impressive costume in the nativity pageant, you're right. That's not your thing. But he'll be a crazy-good narrator. You love history, and you'll teach that kid everything there is to know about Bethlehem in the year AD 1." I smiled.

There are things about mothering and about homemaking that I am decidedly not good at, but the Lord has given me my own set of talents and I bring those to the task. **Lesson learned:** *It's okay to bring a costume-less sheep to the nativity pageant.*

## March 14

Will had taken Liam out to the hall during sacrament meeting because I was flustered and needed a break. I sat in my pew, observing women as they interacted with their children. Looking around, I wondered why all the other women in the room seemed to be such natural mothers. Was it an easy decision for them to have children? Did they always have mothering instincts? Why did they seem to just get it, and why was it so hard for me?

Right then and there, the Spirit taught me. I learned that the call to motherhood, like any commandment, is easier for some to respond to than others. Neither an innate desire nor a natural capacity to mother is a precondition for being a Mormon woman, though it can certainly feel that way! What the women in that chapel that day did have in common was faithfulness. They had answered the charge first given to Adam and Eve to multiply and replenish the earth and were being blessed to do the job well because of their obedience.

This recognition of motherhood as a commandment enabled an important shift in my thinking in the weeks that followed. Instead of mourning for the professional path that I had left, I thanked Heavenly Father for the opportunity to have had a career doing something I enjoyed—even if for just a short time—before it came time for me to assume the principal job to which I was foreordained. I also find peace in knowing that, while motherhood is my current calling, it will not be my last. I am confident that the Lord has other personal and professional opportunities in store for me.

My initial response was not as faithful as Mary of Nazareth's ("Behold, the handmaid of the Lord") or as trusting as Nephi's when called to build a ship ("Whither shall I go that I may find ore to molten, that I may make tools?"), but I said "yes," committing to the Lord to do the best I can. **Lesson learned:** *Motherhood is a calling, one that I accept and reaccept in faith every day.*

## June 21

I sat on California Avenue having appetizers with my former boss, a DC rock star who was in Palo Alto for a conference. Since her time at the White House, she had gone on to lead a prominent nonprofit organization and was thriving professionally. Her résumé was breathtaking and her network enviable. She was put together, smart, savvy, and in demand; she struck me as someone who was, well, fulfilled. I couldn't help but compare our life situations. On the way home, I let myself feel very unimpressive even though I knew better.

Yes, it sounds odd, but a few days later, I looked up the word *fulfillment* in the dictionary. I stumbled across a definition that read, "satisfaction or happiness as a result of fully developing one's abilities or character"[2] and I liked it. If fulfillment is the happy destination we arrive at having fully developed our abilities and character, I thought to myself, then I know of no surer way to fulfillment, for me, than the path of motherhood.

When I was pregnant, family, friends, and even strangers would stop me and say, "Enjoy yourself now because life is about to get really hard." I shrugged off these comments. "Hard?" I would think to myself. "Ha, I've done hard before. I served a mission. I survived graduate school. I've worked eighty-hour weeks." You can imagine how humbled I was to realize that motherhood is an entirely different brand of "hard," harder than all the other types I had experienced before. Who knew, for example, that pacing the stretch of a nursery hundreds of times a night while bouncing a baby to sleep would require such patience (and such strong arms)? Who knew that there would be days when, caught up in caring for my child, I wouldn't eat or shower until five in the afternoon?

Motherhood daily tests and enlarges my intellectual, physical, emotional, and spiritual capacities, asking me to stretch myself in ways far beyond what would ever be required by any other role. It is not only changing what I can do but who I am, smoothing the edges of a prideful, impatient, and sometimes selfish character that is eager for, though not always welcoming of, the refinement.

Motherhood, then, is not just fulfilling in the moments when a child finally eats a bite of broccoli or completes his first piano recital or gives his first talk in church. These milestones are gratifying and worthy of celebration, but motherhood is fulfilling in a much more significant way. In the eternal narrative, we who choose motherhood are fully developing our abilities and character as women and qualifying ourselves to return to our first home. **Lesson learned:** *Motherhood now fulfills me—and will fulfill me eternally—in a way that no other job could.*

Do I have fond memories of my time at the White House? Yes. Do I wonder what could have happened had I stayed on the professional trajectory I was on? Absolutely. But as I learn to embrace my new role and find fulfillment in it, it becomes easier to look back at that period of my life, not with longing, but with peace. Driving that decision is the most compelling promise I can imagine—that if I invest where it matters most now, I can qualify to live eternally with my husband, my children, and my God.

In the meantime, I keep by my bed a promise that means more to me than perhaps any other. On a well-worn copy of my patriarchal blessing, halfway down the page, there are six words that stand out, as if in bold. They read: "You will be a successful mother." Not "You will be a decent mother," or "You will do more good than harm," but "You will be a successful mother." To a prescient Heavenly Father and an inspired stake patriarch, I am grateful for that promise. And with every diaper changed, every feeding complete, and every good night's sleep, I believe it more and more.

# "WHAT DO YOU DO?"

*by Jill Tanner*

The waiting room in a Manhattan fertility clinic holds a diverse group. Prestigious Wall Street executives, illustrious artists and actresses, gay women, single women, successful lawyers, and fashion designers are all checking their Blackberries, reading magazines that don't interest them, and doing everything they can to avoid eye contact with each other as they wait for the nurse to call their name. Some carry Louis Vuitton handbags stuffed with legal briefs and stock reports; others wear comfortable Tory Burch flats so they can walk back to their Central Park West classic-six apartment. The sleepy-eyed artist is nodding off in her chair after waking up early to catch the D train from Brooklyn, and the Broadway star still has makeup smudges left under her eyes from last night's production. Although they come from different backgrounds, they're all in the same room pursuing the same goal: motherhood.

What am I doing in this waiting room? Calling in my next patient to teach her how she'll inject herself with hormones promptly at 9:00 p.m.

I was a newly graduated registered nurse with a young face, ecstatic about my recent cross-country move to the Big Apple and a little apprehensive about working next to some of the nation's top reproductive endocrinology physicians. The majority of our patients were over thirty-five, with many into their forties. They had impressive résumés, great careers, and grand experiences. In the eye of society, they had arrived. Yet, at some point, they decided that whatever they had wasn't enough. Something had been missing in their lives that couldn't be bought with money or demanded with fame. They wanted to be mothers. The maternal instinct that many of them had ignored most of their lives was taking over. Going through fertility treatments is difficult on many levels: physical, emotional, financial, and even social, yet these women were willing to sacrifice it all to obtain a goal that they hoped would bring them the ultimate happiness and fulfillment. President Gordon B. Hinckley said, "It is not going to matter very much how much money you made, what kind of a house you lived in, what kind of a car you drove, the size of your bank account—any of those things. . . . The only things you will take with you, when all is said and done, are your family relationships."[3]

My experiences with these patients confirmed my belief that we find the most fulfillment in the institution of the family and our bonds with others.

A few years later, I became pregnant for the first time myself. I had always wanted to be a mother but was quite naïve about the gritty details of my new role. I will never forget my first night home from the hospital with my newborn. My mother, husband, and I stayed awake from midnight to six in the morning, cramped in our tiny studio apartment with a screaming baby. She cried nonstop the whole night. I tried swaddling, rocking, nursing, giving her a pacifier, and singing—nothing would console her. I remember shedding many tears myself that evening as I stood by her crib and looked out the window at the city lights, wondering why I had never heard other mothers talk of experiences like this one. I was crying for my inadequacy, questioning my decision to be a mother, doubting my ability to care for a fussy baby, and wondering what would happen to my relationship with my husband. Would we ever be able to do the things we enjoyed together before my daughter was born, like going out to dinner or a show? Would I even be able to shower? I had always been told that children would bring me more joy than any other thing in my life. I was feeling a lot of emotions, but joy was not one of them.

The night eventually ended; time passed. We survived the colicky newborn stage and met new challenges, like getting our baby to sleep through the night and figuring out how my talents and skills could be useful in my role as a mother. Our fussy newborn turned into a (mostly) delightful infant. The crying spells that she had every evening tapered off, and she began cooing and giggling. Even though mothering remained difficult, I began to experience the joy that others had promised—the joy only a mother feels when her baby smiles for the first time or claps her hands.

When my daughter was seven months old, we said goodbye to New York City and moved eighty miles north to New Haven, Connecticut, where my husband would pursue an MBA. We left behind a network of friends and colleagues and the identity we had created for ourselves, so I had to redefine myself to all our new acquaintances. During the orientation festivities, which I often attended with our daughter, my husband's classmates asked me, "So what do *you* do?" Initially, I found myself telling stories about the fertility clinic and my school experience and my future educational and professional aspirations in an attempt to justify my accomplishments and goals. But, while my previous life was important to me, my new role as a mother was the most significant. Once people found out I was staying at home with my daughter, many would reply with the signature head tilt and a "that's nice." The subject would return to their visions and plans to change the world. I'd sway with my daughter in my arms as they went on, waiting for a chance to mention how my daughter just learned how to eat solid foods and was only waking up once at night. Those opportunities never came. My own insecurities as a mother left me feeling that maybe what I was doing was not enough.

Ironically, it was through my husband's experience at business school that I overcame these insecurities. One of the benefits of my husband attending the Yale School of Management was the roster of prominent and distinguished guest speakers that addressed his class weekly. We often chatted over dinner about the stories he had heard at talks given in his class. Many of these speakers were at the peaks of their careers. They shared their experiences and tried to give direction to my husband's classmates, all of whom were on their own paths to success. From our point of view, it seemed that the majority of these speakers could be categorized into one of two groups. Either they were wealthy and successful and regretted neglecting and possibly destroying their family relationships in their quest to become so, or they were wealthy and successful and were now trying to find happiness by giving away their money to help others, through non-profits or humanitarian work. Like many of my patients at the fertility clinic, the speakers' focus on temporal things had ended with a search for happiness elsewhere.

These experiences and observations confirmed my belief that my life has a greater purpose. While many seek happiness through worldly accomplishments, I know that life's true "success" is found in my own home. This perspective, now accompanied by intuition and passion, helps me to maintain my sense of purpose, even in the mundane tasks. While my mothering self is constantly evolving, learning, and trying to improve, I've found that I'm happiest and most successful when I'm able to incorporate my passions into my mothering. Whether it's finding time to sew dresses for my girls, reading them a favorite book about a subject I love, practicing my photography skills on them, or attempting to cook them a healthy meal, the joy I have felt as a mother is sweeter than any other joy I have ever experienced. Hearing my baby's giggle and seeing my toddler discover new things confirms how blessed my life as a mother is.

So "what do *I* do?" I am copresident of an organization that has the potential to shape souls and inspire others. I am a teacher, a nurturer, an example, and a support. I heal wounds and wipe tears; I change diapers, I sing songs. I read and laugh. I have a goal of raising children into amazing individuals of character and influence. I am a mother.

"What do *you* do?"

# TEACH THESE SOULS TO FLY

*by Lia Collings*

As I watched the German countryside bump slowly past my train window, I had the unsettling sense that I was being watched—and that the watcher was my sister. "What?" I asked, peering over the head of the baby in my lap. My sister hesitated, her pale, freckled cheeks flushing carnation pink. "Well," she mumbled, now looking everywhere but at me. "So if you don't mind my asking," she began again. As I watched the color spread from her cheeks to her neck, I wondered what question could possibly cause such discomfiture. "Why . . ." she finally blurted, "why would anyone want to be a mom?"

I jerked my head, blinking. If she had leaped across our train car and boxed my ears, I would have been less surprised. My sister, a recently returned missionary from the Germany Munich Mission, had been living with me, my husband, and our three little girls in Frankfurt for five weeks. Months before, when I told her we were going to Germany for my husband to take a language immersion course, she had insisted on coming along. She didn't think much of my ability to navigate three small children through a foreign country on my own. "You will *die*," she predicted. So she bought herself a plane ticket for a two-month pleasure trip with her three darling nieces.

But the trip was not always pleasurable, and the nieces not always darling.

At first I took her question as a thinly veiled complaint. Sure, the first month of our sojourn hadn't been *totally* idyllic. No one liked to live six people deep in a two-room apartment for a summer. I could think of a better use for the twenty minutes we spent stacking and unstacking mattresses at the beginning and end of each day. And it was a challenge to keep a tiny European fridge stocked for three adults and three children. But we were in *Germany*! We had floated on a riverboat past the famous Frankfurt skyline! Dressed the girls in princess dresses and visited the Neuschwanstein castle! Toured downtown Munich and sung with the Glockenspiel! *This* was exciting motherhood—what did she have to complain about? Hadn't *I* been the one with one child strapped to my back, one buckled in my stroller, and one clinging to my leg? Hadn't *I* been the one to silence all the tantrums and petty squabbles? Hadn't *I* masterminded the clean-up of multiple potty-related incidents in disgusting U-Bahn bathrooms? Hadn't *I* . . . .

Ah. I started to see where she was coming from.

"What do you mean?" I asked, tossing my hair over my shoulder and hefting the baby from my lap to the floor. I stayed doubled over to examine the carpet's small white-flowered pattern in a ridiculous effort to hide my face from my sister. "Well, my friend Betsy has been staying with her sister and nieces too, and we just can't figure out . . ." Great. Talking over my lousy life with the BFF. "What do you have to look forward to every day? How do you bear the monotony? Why do you even get up in the morning when no matter what you try to do, you have these kids in the way?"

I felt my body stiffen and my blood rise. Was *that* all she had seen for the last five weeks? Through all the museums, the playgrounds, the Gutenberg and Brothers Grimm birthplaces, she had absorbed only my logistical difficulties? Snatching my baby back from the floor, I sat up straight and stared at her a moment. I struggled to gain my composure but failed. I finally shot back with a flustered, defensive answer—a haughty jumble of idealistic platitudes on the order of finding one's life in losing it for another. She dropped the subject.

I didn't. I thought about the question for months. Why would anyone want to be a mom? From the outside, especially the up-close-and-personal outside that my sister saw, mothering *could* appear to be nothing more than fits and fights, dirty noses, and dirty everything else—no matter the castles-and-fairy-tales sheen I had put on it. To the casual observer, the way I visited those castles—burdened with children on every square inch of my body—might represent motherhood more generally. Mothers, it would seem, were restrained and restricted, held back and weighed down. And yet, excepting the occasional bad day, I didn't feel that way at all about my life as a mother.

Many months after my sister asked me this question, I saw the answer. It lay in a painting on the cover of a book my husband brought home from the library. I couldn't take my eyes off it. "What is that!" I asked, excitedly taking the book from him. My eyes ran eagerly over the image before searching the jacket for the painting's title. I let out an involuntary cry of elation when I found it: *Teach These Souls to Fly* by William Blake. I flipped back to the painting, captivated by the world of this mother and child.

The beige muscles swelling across the mother's back inspired my admiration first. A woman with such strength could perform any labor she chose. Yet the curve of her shoulder introduced a steady softening that ended in a touch on the child's elbow. I saw the same combination of force and persuasion in the look she gave her child. This mother seemed in the same instant both to command and to invite, to compel, and to persuade.

I found the odd trajectory of the mother's flight as intriguing as the paradoxes of her person. She was definitely flying—that was clear by the way her robes hugged her body before swirling away. But her torso twisted back toward her child.

An outsider like my sister might have seen in this mother a picture of how children hamper and restrain. What heights could such a woman *not* have attained, had she been free to pursue the course she had started?

The question could be asked about most mothers. Watching this one—a woman whose strength convinced me she would fly despite the restraints—brought to mind many real-life examples: the mother who during her teensy student-apartment years resolved to learn all there was to know about house plants and went on to teach lessons on the subject; the pastry-loving mother who set a goal to bake one hundred pies, met her goal two years later, and became a master pie-maker in the process; the wife of an emergency medicine doctor who determined that her family would "be prepared" and gave regular workshops on the subject. These women flew, but none of them performed a solo air show. When I heard the urban gardener's three-year-old explain the repotting procedure for philodendrons, the pastry chef's two-year-old critique the flakiness of his pie crust, and the preparedness guru's four-year-old extol the virtues of powdered milk, I knew that in all these women's aeronautics, their children, whether they knew it or not, flew too.

The child in the painting definitely *didn't* know. He stared blankly toward me, not his mother. His chubby toddler arms barely reached past his head, and his feet rose behind him like two lazy balloons. While his mother seemed wholly devoted to some noble end, the child appeared merely present. This child flew only because his mother pulled him, but, like most children, he seemed oblivious to what his mother did for him.

I saw in this half-conscious little soul a reflection of my own children. Try as I might to expose the girls to classical music, they still preferred *Disney Princess Greatest Hits Volume III* to Bach's *Mass in B Minor*. They still craved preservative-laden chicken nuggets to my garden-fresh ratatouille, even though I had drawn neat little chalkboard diagrams to explain how my cooking was really much more tasty, nutritious, and eco-friendly. And I wasn't very amused at my daughter's response when a coworker at my husband's law firm asked, "If I go to work, and my wife goes to work, and your daddy goes to work, then what does your mommy do all day?" "Oh," she responded, shrugging. "She just makes my lunch." Like the child in the painting, my children had no idea how their mother struggled to keep them aloft.

Perhaps my sister had noticed this in them too. Why forego the funds and endure the hassle to raise them to new heights when my children would be content on the ground? Why not provide them with a bare-bones version of what they needed and spend the rest of my energies on myself?

Now seated at the dining room table where I could better study the image, I propped my face in both fists and mentally smiled at my sister for asking such questions. As I watched the flight of this mother-child pair, I thought of how my sister—or any outsider—*couldn't* know about motherhood until she experienced it herself. I didn't think that my sister could know that the ignorance I saw in the child's face could also be innocence.

In humility, he let his mother pull him—just as my children let me—proving him everything King Benjamin required: "submissive, meek, humble, patient, full of love, and willing to submit to all things which [his mother saw] fit to inflict upon him" (Mosiah 3:19). In devoting my days and nights to my children—the sort of individuals the Savior had said made up the kingdom of heaven—I might teach them all that I knew, but they would teach me many, much more important lessons through their childlike nature. We would lift each other. Considering the symbiotic relationship between this mother and child, I found the use of the plural "these" in Blake's title to be profound: *Teach These Souls to Fly*.

It would be impossible to convey to my sister all the flying I did as a mother. I could mention that I had taught my daughter to read, but my sister couldn't know how it made my own soul soar to see the wonder in my daughter's face when she read her first book. My sister could marvel to hear my three-year-old identify a particular waltz on the radio, but she couldn't experience the earlier lift of listening to Strauss for hours with that little one. Until she turned back to teach a child she loved to fly, my sister couldn't know the profound joy I felt to hear my children lovingly and patiently teaching one another.

The interesting thing about this painting was that it wasn't particularly beautiful or technically impressive. Still, the longer I looked at it, the more the mother in me responded to it. As I watched the young child in the painting, I felt with a sense of urgency that he had entered a fallen world, and, but for the guiding hand of his mother, he would sink into the blacks and reds toward the bottom of the painting. The protective shield of light and truth his mother provided for him—a safe haven from the world around them—relieved me. I felt a kinship with her efforts to guide her child into the airy blue expanses that this world also extends.

This powerful woman reminded me of Elder M. Russell Ballard's counsel: "As mothers in Israel, you are your [children's] first line of defense against the wiles of the world."[4] I couldn't provide my children better protection against darkness than to teach their souls to fly above it, to teach them to rise above the middling, the tawdry, the base, and follow me into the beautiful, the exalting, the holy. Satan ensures that the reds and blacks always will be there. In her position as her child's first defense, the mother must identify the blues and yellows, and she must teach a child how to fly to them. "Teach these souls to fly"—the sacred duty entrusted to mothers, a sacred opportunity afforded to women.

I finally laid down the book with a feeling of reverent awe. "Who *wouldn't* want to be a mom?" I wondered. A career in motherhood had its elements of drudgery, but so did any other. What other career could claim as its end product the elevation of a human soul? Not just the enlightening of a mind or the development of a body, but the improvement of every aspect of a vibrant child of God? I, at least, wanted to be a mother because I believed, with President Harold B. Lee, that the most important work I would ever do would be within the walls of my own home. I chose to be a mother because I wanted to teach souls to fly.

# GOLD STARS AND SMILEY FACES

*by Gretchen Cheney*

Sitting on paper exam sheets in the doctor's office, I wait for the test results, pleading within myself, "Please be positive, please, please . . ." I throw the *People* magazine I have been attempting to read on the counter next to me and wistfully stare out the window at the students passing by. I see dog-walkers, professors, and clusters of undergrads walking around, savoring this cloudless September afternoon. Laughing, chatting, greeting old friends, they look free from any kind of concern right now. But I'm a mess. I wipe my sweaty palms on the paper I've creased and torn under my shifting legs.

My thoughts drift to the miscarriage I experienced last year. I never thought I would have trouble getting pregnant; my mom had eight kids with no problem. I always pictured myself conceiving the first month we tried. Now, almost two and a half years and thirty negative pregnancy tests later, I fear that I will never be able to have my own children. As I offer a silent prayer of desire to be blessed with a child, a loud knock at the door interrupts me. "Come in," I respond. A somber-looking nurse enters, carrying a clipboard and shaking her head. "Well?" I implore.

"Mrs. Cheney," she says, "the test was positive. How would you like to proceed? Is this good news?" My heart explodes with joy at the news and I want to break out in a celebratory dance, but before I can answer the nurse's question with a resounding "yes," she quickly adds, "You do have options." She is clearly concerned. What is she talking about?

"Yes, this is *very* good news," I answer with a broad smile on my face. I can't wait to tell my husband; he'll be ecstatic!

"Oh, that's good . . . you are so young, and are you in school?" the nurse asks. I am taken aback. The thought never entered my mind that having a child could be considered bad news.

This incident was the first time I saw how others might react to the idea of me having children: with more concern than congratulations. But motherhood, at this point, was more important to me than strangers' approval. That's saying a lot for someone like me who grew up doing anything for an extra smiley face or gold star.

I am somewhat of a perfectionist. When I was in elementary school, I would meticulously outline and color all of the little pictures on the sides of my worksheets, even if it wasn't required. A simple spelling worksheet would become a multicolored masterpiece. I never once missed an assignment and would cry bitter tears if I ever got less than a 100 percent. I did extra credit just to earn the highest A I could—I didn't just want an A, I wanted a super A. And I loved, loved, loved getting praise from my teachers. Some would say I was sort of a brown-noser. My old class photos don't offer much evidence to refute that assertion—you can find me sitting on my teacher's lap in just about every one of them. If that doesn't say "kiss-up," I'm not sure what does.

I continued as a teacher's pet throughout high school and college, where I never once received as much as a B in any of my classes. Was I extra smart? Gifted? Certainly not! I struggled for those As. I had to find tutors and ask for extra help. School was never easy for me—far from it. But I loved that praise! I loved the feeling I got when I received that A. An A meant that I was special, that I stood out. I always wanted to do my best.

In college I decided to pursue a degree in elementary education. I don't care what anybody says; teaching is the hardest, most challenging job there is. Teachers work around the clock planning, grading, fretting about their students. Meeting the needs of thirty students at a time is no small task, something I learned while fulfilling my grueling student-teaching requirement. I also saw why so many teachers stick around year after year, despite their small paychecks. They do it for the hugs, the letters of appreciation, the smiles. They do it to make a difference in children's lives and to watch them learn and grow. They also enjoy the occasional recognition that they are teaching and sacrificing for the next generation. Since I've always loved praise and high fives, it's no wonder that I chose teaching as a profession.

Even so, my students could never admire me as much as they admire their mothers, nor could I teach them as much as they learn in their homes. When a child writes about his hero, it's often his mother. When a child is hurt, she wants her mother. When a child creates something he is proud of, he says, "I can't wait to show my mom." With my elementary education degree, I have taught children in various capacities over the last few years. I have taught at summer camps, a gymnastics gym, a preschool, and in private homes as a nanny. The number one thing I learned from each of those jobs: *kids need their moms!*

I've seen the importance of mothers in my academic research too. For my final college project, I wrote a paper about gifted children. I talked to children and parents who participated in the gifted and talented programs at several schools. Sure enough, I found that almost all of these children had parents who were actively involved in their child's education. They were there for the children when they got home from school, they helped them with their homework, and they read to them at night.

As I made these observations in the classroom, I decided I didn't really want to teach other people's kids and receive their hugs and appreciation (although that was great). I wanted to teach my own kids.

My own children would receive the benefits of my time and planning. I wanted to be their hero. I have little doubt that I could have picked any profession I wanted and done well at it, with sufficient effort. I *am* a hard worker, I believe in myself, and I love to make other people proud of me. But I know that I have picked the profession—motherhood—that will allow me to feel the most satisfaction and influence the children most important to me.

Does the world applaud my devotion to my kids? In my experience, no. I have been asked why I would sacrifice my talents to stay home with my children. Even other moms have asked why I don't do more for myself. How do I survive the drudgery of changing the soiled sheets of a potty-training toddler, they wonder, or the grunt work of cleaning up peas that have been smashed into the carpet? Yes, the job title of "mother" does require you to take on some not-too-pleasant duties, but my job description also includes these tasks: play, discover, and laugh. I was lucky enough to have the choice to stay home with my children (I know not everyone does), and because I chose to work for my children, I am going to enjoy it by having the right attitude toward my job.

My appetite for approval hasn't vanished, but the applause of strangers seems so shallow compared to the sweetness of my little boy wrapping his arms tightly around me and whispering, "Mommy." I have also felt, on several occasions, that my Heavenly Father is pleased with the decision I have made; He has reassured me that I am doing what's best for my family.

After the nurse told me the *good* news, I could hardly feel the clinic floor beneath my feet. I grabbed my purse and walked onto the elevator in a daze. "I am going to be a mom. I am going to be a mom," I repeated in my head as I ran to the law school to tell my husband the news. When I saw the look on my husband's face and we embraced, I couldn't remember a happier moment in our marriage. This is what we had wanted for so long! We celebrated by buying a pregnancy magazine and looking up baby names until the wee hours of the morning.

The birth of our son led me to discover a depth of love I didn't know existed. I never thought I could feel such concern or adoration for one little boy. I have decided to pursue a career the world seems not to appreciate. Yet when I pause to take stock of what I have given up and what I have gained, I find that the decision wasn't even a close call. Could I use an additional paycheck? Sure. But I'd rather miss a paycheck than my son's first word. Do I miss the attention from the world? Not as much as I miss my son when we're apart. And when we're together, I tend to forget all about those gold stars and extra smiley faces anyway.

# "NOW IS THE WINTER OF OUR DISCONTENT, MADE GLORIOUS SUMMER"

*by Keely Knudsen*

I *am in the waiting room again.*

It was nearly one year ago in this same building that I saw her for the first time. She was lying inside the transparent box that kept her warm and protected from the elements. Her legs were folded stiffly, creasing her new body in half, her sweet misshapen feet lingering permanently by her ears. She had an open spine then—one that had grown outside of her back as her body was forming itself in the womb. A team of surgeons had just enclosed the nerve endings safely inside her body, and fresh, moist wrappings protected the affected area. So she was on her side, my little girl. All the time, those first several weeks, only on her side. The nerves pushed back inside her body were dead, with no real way to connect where they needed to go . . . and that meant our little baby girl, four weeks early and six pounds total, had paralysis. As I gazed at my daughter inside the transparent box, I felt a steel in my soul, a confidence that I had never before known—she and I were going to make it.

*In the waiting room, there is a snack area. It's stocked*

*with peanut butter in small, round individual casements and graham crackers, two to a package. These snacks were my feast, once upon a time, and filet mignon could not have rivaled the manna that snack was to me then.*

It was nearly one year ago—my husband's birthday. We were dining at a restaurant in downtown New Haven, eating food so delicious that even though I had begun to have contractions fewer than five minutes apart, I stayed for dessert. I had already scheduled a C-section at a hospital four hours and several states away. This was not the time and certainly not the place that this was supposed to happen. We concluded the birthday dinner in reverie from the remarkable cuisine, and I informed my husband we ought to just swing by the nearest hospital and see if perhaps they could make these silly contractions stop.

I was admitted to Yale-New Haven hospital. Within minutes, I was on the phone with the Children's Hospital of Philadelphia, best in the world for babies with my daughter's condition, and the hospital that had conducted our prenatal surgery trial. The consensus was *stop the labor, if you can.* The lime from the ceviche still delighted my tongue, and little did I realize that the dinner at the restaurant truly was my last supper. The labor stopped (*oh, true apothecary, thy drugs are quick*), but only as long as the harsh medicine coursed through my veins. Each let up of the medicine led to a prompt return of the contractions. Three days later, I was still in the same local hospital, having consumed nothing but the not-delicious, not-satisfying, but certainly bladder-filling IV solution, and the decision was made to deliver her via C-section to avoid disrupting the large membrane sac of spinal nerves on her lower back. We were wheeled into a sterile, large, echo-y room. Bright lights lit the white floors, walls, and ceilings, and Bon Jovi's "Living on a Prayer" blared from the radio. A large team of doctors and students shouted business-and-casual comments, dressed in blue-green surgical masks and with caps that reminded me of my Grandma Ruthie when she would adorn herself for a shower. My arms were to be outstretched to the side as they ripped her from my belly, and I pondered the final pose of my Savior as I lay there—my Savior, the one who had gotten me through this nightmare pregnancy, who would surely get me through all that lay ahead.

I didn't see her face. I didn't hear her cry. She made it to mortality and hung out for a good half day before I could set eyes on her. Others had seen her—my husband, for one, and many strangers employed by the hospital. But I hadn't. Hours after the delivery, I lay in the hospital bed, wired, desperately clinging to the lists of care I had researched concerning her condition. And now, *enter stage right* peanut butter in a cute, tiny little casement and two graham crackers in a shiny cellophane wrapper. Since my last supper, it had also been three days until I was made new again. When I ate the snack that the nurse delivered, I thought I had never tasted anything finer than those graham crackers and peanut butter. The Spanish food from the candlelit table for two paled in comparison at this delight, this rare treat, this food fit for a king. Peanut butter and graham crackers.

*The nurse comes out to fill me in. Evidently, anesthesia has been administered to my daughter, and she's just fine. Two incisions have been made in each of her heels, and the surgery has been underway successfully for the last fifteen minutes. She expects to give another update in a little bit.*

The graham crackers were a real theme. I remember snacking on them in the specialist's waiting room when I had my appointment to learn why my AFP blood scores were so high. I consider food intake when I am not pregnant, but when I am, all bets are off. I am a cow, and I embrace that role. Food anywhere is an invitation to continue growing the belly beyond the necessary range. Granola bars and graham crackers were some real favorites, and that specialist's office always carried the promise of such treats, regardless of whatever messy or downright horrifying news they had to tell you there.

I knew that place. I had grown to detest the very building. I would drive by it and consciously look away, or worse, erupt into tears if I got close enough to it. I was actively fighting the tears just entering that building to have the AFP scores checked this time around. I had a lump in my throat that caused me physical pain in my efforts to not crumble. After all, the last time I had been to that building was when they told me my second child, Emma Hope, had died in the womb due to Turner's Syndrome. I ended up laboring and delivering our dead baby, and the grief that it caused led me into new depths. I discovered crevices inside of me where the pain sank so deeply—places that I never knew before existed. You see, Emma's body had been developing with her organs outside her body, and she had a 1 percent chance at life. But I had promised the Lord in the temple that I was good for it—that I would raise her and make whatever sacrifices were required of me to do so. I felt trusted by Him to take on the grand challenge . . . and then she died. What a blessing that experience was to prepare me, as I ate the graham crackers furiously in the waiting room and tried to fight off the palpable memories of that intense grief and loss.

The specialist called me in. Spina bifida. That is what the doctor told me. Spina bifida. I took my planner out and grabbed the only piece of paper I could find and began scribbling as I shot questions his way. The man never looked at me as he spouted off descriptors such as *paralyzed, wheelchair bound, depressed, high divorce rates for parents, learning disabilities, brain surgery, troublesome for siblings,* and the list went on. I looked up at him, frustrated. "But is the baby going to live?" The doctor paused. Then he stammered, "Well . . . if you decide to have the baby . . . there are no lung and heart issues involved in spina bifida. However, the quality of life is so challenged for these individuals that 95 percent of mothers carrying babies with this birth defect opt for therapeutic abortion." I zipped up my notes in my calendar and stuffed them into the bag with the cellophane cracker wrappers and made a beeline for the waiting room, straight through the door, then down the stairs, then out the sliding doors, into the parking lot, and into my car just in time for the hysteria and grief to completely overtake me. I spoke out loud, I remember, as I drove north on 95. But I have no idea what I said or to whom I was speaking. Perhaps I was praying. I couldn't pick up my one- and four-year-old from the babysitter. I could barely breathe. I had to at least control myself before facing them.

I have a friend who lives around the corner from me. She is like a sister. She has experienced loss to its fullest and takes challenges on with analytic fervor and a proactivity that rivals the abilities of any world leader. I trust her with my life. I drove to her house. I ran to her front door, sobbing, rang her doorbell, and banged on the door, wishing I could see some sort of irony or humor in the drama of it all. I couldn't. The door never opened, so I fell on the bench on her front porch in a heap and heaved my sorrow to whomever would listen. Mambo, the family dog, the one I had house-sat for years even before I was married, came to me in my need. She and I sat there in the elements, and she held me as I cried and comforted my soul.

*The secretary calls out, "Wynter Knudsen?" (She pronounced it correctly—Danish hard K and all.) The surgery is complete, and the doctor will come out soon to give me the full update.*

In our efforts to educate ourselves on the birth defect and our options, my husband and I became members of a study called MOMS (Management of Myelomeningocele Studies) which, I kid you not, took place at CHOP (Children's Hospital of Philadelphia). And CHOPping MOMS wasn't a misrepresentation of what the study offered: an intense in-utero surgery, which would slit the pregnant belly vertically to reveal the baby, sew up the membrane sac of the baby's spine, then sew Mommy back up, all in the *hopes* that over the following weeks, the elements would not further alter the function of the exposed membrane. We qualified, but we were randomized into the control group part of the study. Further research indicated there were no other options for the in-utero surgery in North America, but we did come across a doctor in Germany trying out a new procedure.

The flight to Germany was crowded, and my husband

and I were not seated next to each other. I watched the rain fall to the pavement from my window seat as my tears mirrored the window's trail of water. We had left our two children behind in the States in an effort to give Wynter the best chances at life. The surgery would have meant a four-month stay overseas for me, and she would have been born in Germany. The anticipation was unbearable for me as the plane began its descent to the Frankfurt airport.

Before the first full day away from our girls was complete, we had met our German doctor, received an impromptu ultrasound, and learned that his surgery was not recommended on our particular baby. In great Abrahamic relief, my husband and I enjoyed a second honeymoon in Germany and enthusiastically returned to the States. At this point, we felt we had done all we could do. Now, we would simply sit in Life's great waiting room . . . and eat graham crackers and peanut butter.

*The nurse, who just left the chair sitting next to mine, lights up when she speaks about the angelic disposition of my daughter. Everyone does; this is no news to me. "I have never seen a sweeter little girl," she says.*

I was trying a new recipe one afternoon when I heard a sound that startled me. It sounded like choking. I dropped my culinary battle mid-scene and ran to my four-month-old "with special needs," who was purposely sequestered from my two-year-old (who loves the baby and must demonstrate that love in short, brutish, physical spurts some might call attacks). The choking noise came again. I was no sooner jabbing my hooked finger in the baby's mouth when I realized, stopping myself: she's not choking, *she's laughing.* There was a smile of delight on her face, complete with daddy's dimples, and she looked up at me, this time finding great humor in my dramatic entrance—or perhaps the unexpected finger in the mouth—in any case, she took a deep belly breath and guffawed, shoulders rolling forward, the whole nine yards. She laughed. She laughed then, and she still laughs, harder than my other two girls, and more often. My nearly one-year-old girl with spina bifida has a better sense of humor than the rest of us.

And so she has revealed her exceptional spirit to us. But this is not all: uncanny events have transpired in our lives since her birth. Many of the dreams on our lists have come true. Financial, career, and artistic pursuits have gone through the roof. Happiness in our family has never been greater. I have even more joy and a heightened perspective of life. We have a new perspective on bodies and health and a new definition for what it is to be *normal*. Wynter makes me grateful. I am grateful in all ways, but, most of all, I am grateful that I get to keep her.

*I am entering the long, sterile hospital corridor leading to Wynter, walking toward my daughter whose surgery was performed in hopes of her someday walking toward me. She is wearing yellow hospital pajamas, coming out of anesthesia slowly, groggily. Her two legs are molded in large, white plaster casts from her toes to her hips, and I realize that it will only take a roll of toilet paper to complete her costume for this evening's Halloween party. She and I snuggle and stare at each other. Even though she is weary and spent, nothing masks the twinkle in her eye.*

There will be countless times over my life that I will be sitting in the waiting room, waiting for Wynter. Next month, Wynter, her Daddy, and I will travel to the Children's Hospital of Philadelphia (a trek we made about every ten days for the first several months, which has now evened out to every three months or so) for a one-year checkup. The doctors will examine her head (although I often think they'd best do that to us adults instead) to ensure she still shows no signs of hydrocephalus (miracle number one). They will examine her kidneys to see if they still function properly (miracle number two). They will also assess her cognitive development to determine whether she really is as smart and exceptional as we think she is, despite her condition (miracle number three). And her un-cast legs, which by then should be fitted into new, tall, purple boots, will be examined to see if one day our little Wynter may, like those multicolored butterflies adorning the sides of the boots, indeed fly.

She makes my heart soar. She completes me in all ways. How much better my life is—how much better—because I chose to identify with the 5 percent of mothers who closed their eyes, took a deep breath, and plunged into the unknown. What a grand relief to know that I can, in a coming day, run to my Heavenly Father's embrace, exclaiming, "I am so glad that I trusted you!"

I'm so glad that *He* trusted *me*.

# THE FIVE-YEAR PLAN

*by Kristy Walker*

I sat in the dark one night, rocking my six-month-old son to sleep. A CD of Primary songs was playing in the background as we glided back and forth in the chair my mother had given to me shortly before my son was born. He had been unusually fussy that day, and I was tired, worn out, and overwhelmed. I put my feet up and closed my eyes, grateful that my son had finally calmed down and the house was still. However, my mind was racing, and I couldn't seem to relax despite my exhaustion. My thoughts drifted to my husband, a busy medical resident who we had barely seen all week. I yearned to be able to spend time with him and to have his help with our baby. I knew he wanted the same thing, but sometimes I felt like I was a single mom. We had recently moved to a new state, and I felt very alone.

I started to think about what had led me to this point—to this moment in the rocking chair where the responsibility and the weight of being a mother was so heavy. I questioned why I felt so inadequate—this was something I was supposed to do, something I had always wanted to do. So why wasn't

I more joyful? I was doing the best I could, but somehow it didn't feel like enough. As a mother I never knew what each new day would bring—would my son by happy, sad, tired, alert, or some kind of mixture of it all? The uncertainty was sometimes difficult for me.

I had always been the girl with the five-year plan. I was motivated, involved, and often recognized for my achievements. From the time I was in high school, I had known exactly what I wanted to do with my life. I was going to attend a university where I would major in political science or communications. I would then complete an internship in Washington, DC, and apply for law school. When I had accomplished these things, I would find a husband, fall in love, and later have a family. It all seemed glamorous, and I thought I would complete these goals, in this order.

Everything changed when I met my husband during my freshman year of college. He came into my life much sooner than I expected. As our relationship progressed, I knew that I needed to make a decision. I had a choice to follow the promptings I was receiving to get married and set my plan in line with what I felt the Lord was telling me to do, or to ignore those promptings and continue on the path I had started. Ultimately I decided to follow the promptings to get married, knowing that my plan would likely deviate dramatically from its original version. I was deeply in love with my husband, and I had faith that everything would work out.

My husband applied to medical school, which ultimately meant my East Coast experience would happen a little sooner than I had anticipated. Shortly before our first anniversary, we packed our few belongings in a moving truck and camped across the country. We were too poor to afford hotels. After a week of campfires, mosquitoes, public showers, the license plate game, and many Church history sites, we arrived at our final destination: New Haven, Connecticut.

Year one of medical school began to engross my husband. Meanwhile, I worked thirty hours a week and took eighteen credits of school each semester so I'd be able to complete my bachelor's degree, while supporting our family. I wasn't about to let go of my education, so I did what was necessary to make that happen.

I took a job working in the hotel industry as a conference and event planner. I enjoyed the variety my job offered day to day. However, a lot of stress was involved in making sure my customers were happy. Did my staff set up the room properly? Was the food served on time? Why isn't the projector working? I started to wonder if what I did on a daily basis meant something to someone and whether I was really contributing anything that mattered.

After completing my bachelor's degree, my husband and I started to discuss the possibility of starting our family. We also heard about some exciting opportunities through the medical school to live internationally for a year. We decided to pursue both options and wait to see what happened. We determined that if I became pregnant, we would forego the international opportunity so I wouldn't give birth in a developing country.

A few months later I was suspicious that I might be pregnant and went to the clinic for a pregnancy test. Though the results took longer than an over-the-counter test, it was free, and we were poor students. A couple of days later, I received a call from the clinic telling me that I was pregnant! Yet I was suspicious that my body was telling me otherwise. In the same day that I learned that I was pregnant, I also had a feeling that I had had a miscarriage. I still had some hope that somehow, someway, I might still be pregnant. I wasn't ready to let go of that hope. I made an appointment with my doctor, and she confirmed that I had indeed miscarried. I was heartbroken. If the Lord had commanded us to multiply and replenish the earth, why was this happening to me? Wasn't He supposed to help us fulfill his commandments? Comfort came one night when I had a dream prompting me that we weren't supposed to start our family at that time, but that we should pursue the other options available to us. Once again I had a choice to make. I could continue to grieve or I could trust that the Lord had a better plan for me.

Six months later, we were packing our belongings into storage and moving to Peru, where we lived for the next ten months. There, my husband worked on medical research, and I took language classes to learn Spanish. The first few weeks I was terrified to leave our apartment by myself. We lived in a safe part of town, but I didn't speak the language and worried about how I'd find my way through unfamiliar streets or communicate if someone spoke to me. I quickly learned that I would need to devote myself entirely to learning Spanish if I hoped to accomplish anything during the time we spent there. I studied many hours each day, and slowly the language started to come. Learning a new language taught me a lot of patience and humility. It was hard. Just when I thought I had mastered a grammar rule, I'd completely draw a blank on how to conjugate a verb or how to speak in the proper tense. I had to humble myself to continue trying to speak the language even though I didn't speak it perfectly.

A few months into our stay, I was approached by a nonprofit organization that was looking for someone to head a summer program teaching English. The students were high-school aged and lived in a shanty town called Las Pampas about forty-five minutes outside of Lima. I was nervous: I had never been a teacher before, and I had no formal training in teaching a language. However, I knew I wanted to do something meaningful during our time in Peru, so I said yes. I will never forget how I felt as I looked out the windows of the crowded city bus and saw the town where I would be volunteering. It was dusty as the bus crept along the dirt road. The houses were small, constructed of cinder blocks and built close together on large, sandy hills. They had tin roofs and no running water. As I watched them slip past the windows of the bus, I felt humble. I had only heard of living conditions such as these before and seeing them firsthand evoked sadness. I also felt extremely grateful for the material blessings I enjoy.

My teaching companion and I reached our destination and yelled, as is the custom, for the bus driver to let us off. We wandered down the hill to a small health post where we would be teaching. We entered the health post and started to set up our classroom in the courtyard. There were no chairs or desks—just hard, dirty cement steps to sit on and whitewashed cinder-block walls. We hung paper to serve as our whiteboard and waited anxiously to see if any students would show up. As we were getting ready to start, I counted sixteen students between the ages of fifteen and eighteen. I started to feel intimidated. I wondered if I'd be able to teach these teenagers anything helpful. Our first lesson was about introductions. By the end of the class, all the students could say, "Hi, my name is ________. What's your name?" The students caught on to the concepts quickly. I returned to this post once a week through the summer. The students were eager to learn: they were not forced to come spend their summer in a classroom, but they chose to be there and they always showed up on time. I grew to love these kids—Ronald, who didn't hesitate to correct my Spanish when I spoke incorrectly, and Winnie, who despite her living conditions always came looking sharp, without a single hair out of place. Each of the students had different personalities, and I really looked forward to the time we spent together. Despite my initial fears about my qualifications, I learned that my desire to teach these kids, coupled with a lot of preparation, helped me to succeed. At least two of these students went on to graduate from high school and pursue additional training at a vocational school and a local university.

The ten months flew by, and the time came for us to load our belongings back into our suitcases and return to the United States. I thought back to our first weeks in the country and had to laugh about how intimidated I was to even leave our apartment. I consider the opportunity I had to learn Spanish, associate with such humble people, and travel throughout the beautiful country of Peru among the most influential experiences of my life. I learned that I could do hard things. I also learned to trust more in the Lord; I learned that He does have a plan for me and that He knows what is best for me. Had I not miscarried, I never would have experienced the personal growth that came as the result of living in a foreign country. Had I not learned Spanish during my time in Peru, I would have struggled with my calling, a few years later, as the Relief Society President of a ward with twenty Spanish-speaking sisters. I know now that the Lord was preparing me to be able to serve these sisters. He had a better plan for me. Part of that plan included motherhood—when my husband and I returned to the United States, I was three months pregnant with our first child.

Motherhood isn't exactly what I expected. If there are moments of pure joy when my children smile for the first time or look to me for comfort when they cry, there are also moments of bone-weary fatigue from night after night of interrupted sleep. I feel, sometimes, as I did those first few weeks in Peru—frightened, unsettled, and unsure of my own abilities. But as I sat in the darkened room that particular night, rocking my firstborn son and reflecting on the path that led me to that point, I was reminded of something I had learned in Peru: I can do hard things with the Lord's help. In the midst of my sense of inadequacy, I remembered too that I didn't have to be qualified to be a good mother—I just had to have the desire and the willingness to work at it.

The five years I had just spent didn't look much like my original five-year plan. And I'm glad they didn't: the Lord had something better in mind for me. Although He didn't prepare me to be successful in the courtroom, He prepared me to become a good mother by teaching me patience and humility. I knew that night as I looked down at my sleeping child that he was a child of God, and that the Lord had entrusted me with the responsibility to raise him in truth and righteousness. As I sat there, a beautiful song came on the CD we were listening to. The words "I feel my Savior's love, in all the world around me. His spirit warms my soul through everything I see" filled the room. I felt the Lord's spirit reminding me that, even though it seemed difficult at times, He would lead and guide me in this work of motherhood, just as He had in other areas of my life. In that dark, quiet night, I experienced one of those tender mercies of the Lord that help us through difficult stretches: the Lord told me unmistakably that I was doing my best, and, while my efforts were far from perfect, they were acceptable to him. I felt the love my Savior has for me and His love for my willingness to take on the important work of a mother. I still don't know everything about being a good mother, but the Lord does. That thought continues to give me hope, as I desire to learn and to provide for my children in His way. I know that as I seek His help and guidance, He blesses me with inspiration. He loves me, He loves my children, and I know that He will help me lead my children in righteousness so that we may all return to his presence someday.

# BUT WE HEEDED THEM NOT

*by Elizabeth Taylor*

W*ould we ever be able to fit everything?* I looked around my room, the light still blazing, at the piles I had been sorting before I fell asleep. It was a hot, muggy night in July, and I squinted at the clock: 1:00 a.m. My soon-to-be husband was starting graduate school on the East Coast and with no furniture to our names, we both ambitiously thought we could fit everything in a 1993 Toyota Corolla and drive the 2,300 miles across the country. But that required a lot of sorting. I assessed the piles and looked at the last box—my running box. It was full of trophies, plaques, ribbons, and medals. I had already separated out the ones that I really cared about and placed them carefully in a shoe box. The rest I figured I didn't need, so they were going to be given away at our next family race. I looked at the shoe box and a thought came to me:

*You don't need to keep that.*

I started, surprised: "But it's small. These are the medals I care most about. This box represents literally hundreds of hours of running."

*Just let it go.*

"Okay," I thought to myself, "but I'll look through it first to make sure I'm okay with that."

*Don't open it*, the thought said. *Just let it go.*

Slowly I picked up my shoebox. Then before I could stop myself, I left my second story apartment, walked around the balcony of the complex, and looked down at the dumpster squatting fifteen feet below. After only a moment I lifted the box over the railing and let it slip from my fingers. Hitting the bags of kitchen trash and college apartment refuse below, the black shoe box bounced open. All I saw through my tear-blurred eyes were ribbons and medals spilling out—state track medals, triathlon medals, and my prized marathon medals—bouncing, then still. My stomach lurched, and I turned, running back to my apartment.

I didn't know why I had thrown away that box, but something about it felt right. Looking back on the experience I've reflected on the scripture: "Yet shall I be glorious in the eyes of the Lord and my God shall be my strength" (1 Nephi 21:5). As I was preparing for marriage, I was moving not only to a new location but into a new stage of life, one where in order to survive—even thrive—I needed to understand that the glory of God matters more than the honors or praise of man. In an action that perhaps only mattered to me, I left behind what the world thought and prepared to live for an eternal reward. I would like to say I was perfect from then on, but leaving the world behind and becoming more like Christ is a constant struggle—one I have learned more about by becoming a mother than by anything else.

My husband, Seth, and I were married in the Salt Lake Temple on August 21, 2008. After our reception, we hopped in our tightly packed car and drove to New Haven, Connecticut. As a newlywed, I was faced with an interesting dilemma. I remembered Sister Beck's talk, "Mothers Who Know" in which she directly counsels that "Mothers who know desire to bear children" and quotes Ezra Taft Benson, saying, "Young couples should not postpone having children."[5] Before I was married that had seemed simple. Now I was faced with reality. I was far from home, didn't know anyone in New Haven, and didn't know much about being pregnant. But my husband and I both felt good about having children and decided to leave it in the Lord's hands. Less than a month later, I was pregnant.

I had thought being pregnant would be fun. I would go along with normal life as my stomach grew bigger and bigger. Wrong. Life was completely different. After one run at two months pregnant where I insisted on doing hill repeats, I almost passed out in the shower. I felt so sick that I had to lie on the bed for hours until I felt better. I stopped running. I was used to being a productive person, but now I struggled to make it to the one class I was taking in order to finish my degree. I took four-hour naps and still slept all night. And I worried what people would think: "Were you planning on having children so quickly?" or "Wow, that was fast." I worried about what Seth's family would think. His dad had told us that it's nice to have a few months to get to know each other. I was supposed to student-teach in the spring, and I remembered one of my teachers saying, "Just don't get pregnant while you are student teaching. It's really hard." I didn't know what the teachers I was working with would think. Suddenly I wasn't sure what *I* thought.

One night in early October, I knelt down on the linoleum floor in the kitchen to ask Heavenly Father for help I desperately needed. I felt alone and bewildered. I didn't even know how or when to go to the doctor. But as I knelt, I remembered Elder Bednar's recent conference address in which he said, "Let me recommend that periodically you and I offer a prayer in which we only give thanks and express gratitude."[6] I hesitated, but knew what I should do. I thanked Heavenly Father for my marriage and that we were sealed as an eternal family. I thanked Him for the child that would be coming to our home and thanked Him for watching over us. As I prayed, I felt true gratitude well up inside of me. I realized that *this* was what I wanted, what my heart and spirit desired: to have a family, to be a wife and to be a mother. This was Heavenly Father's plan and it didn't matter what others thought. This was what was "glorious in the eyes of the Lord" (Isaiah 49:5).

But the battle of leaving the world behind had scarcely begun. For one thing, I struggled to reconcile my desire to be a mother with my love of learning and my interest in teaching. I realize now that the struggle was not between motherhood and teaching, but between what I felt was right and what others expected me to do.

In kindergarten, my teacher asked us to write what we wanted to be on a piece of construction paper and put it on the wall with our pictures. I can still see my smiling face and my childlike handwriting: "When I grow up I want to be a mommy." I had seen how happy my mother was with her nine children and I wanted to do the same. My desire didn't fade with time, but my courage to express it did. As I grew older, I felt like there were too many "what ifs" to go around telling people of my desire to be a mother. "What if I never got married?" "What if I didn't have children?"

So, until I had the chance to be a mother, I focused on my education. I knew from President Hinckley's counsel that it was important to get an education; I also knew I had a gift for academic study. I excelled in high school and was awarded the Gordon B. Hinckley scholarship to BYU. Once at BYU, picking a major was incredibly difficult. I loved everything. I loved learning about cells and enzymes and kingdoms and phyla. I loved leaving the testing center with words like "endoplasmic reticulum" or "apical meristem" running through my head. I loved learning about the human body. I loved the feeling of getting the right answer to a calculus problem after three pages of calculations. And I loved literature and the smell of books. I would occasionally go down to the bottom level of the BYU library and walk through the rows of books, just touching their bindings. I would sometimes stay up until three or four in the morning reading a book that wasn't even required. Things really got confusing when I took a dreaded economics class at BYU and loved it. I didn't know how to pick just one thing to major in, or one thing to "become." After two years of majoring in bioinformatics, I left for a mission to Brazil, where I finally realized which major I wanted to pursue.

I can still remember clearly sitting in front of an investigator and trying with every ounce of energy I had to explain the Apostasy and the Restoration. No matter how hard I tried to get the idea across, she didn't understand. I came home frustrated, feeling that my inability to teach had kept her from learning. I decided that more than anything, I wanted to be able to teach. After my mission, I majored in English teaching. When my husband and I packed up our car and drove to Connecticut, I had one year of college left. Through a series of miracles, I was able to make arrangements to finish my schooling in New Haven, student-teach in Connecticut, and graduate from BYU the next spring. It was obvious to me that Heavenly Father had a hand in directing and helping me finish my education. It wasn't as obvious what I should do next.

Perhaps with my lack of courage to express it, my desire to be a full-time mother *had* faded. Spring semester started, and I began student teaching. While busy teaching, I thought much about my future career. I worried that if I became a full-time mother I would be bored at home, or worse, feel like I was not accomplishing anything. People often asked me where I was going to apply to work the next year. I told them I was having a baby and wasn't looking for anything right away. The next question was always, "When are you going back to work?" I didn't know what to say. I felt it was acceptable in my profession to take a year off to have a baby, but not more. And I loved teaching. I had great mentors who would be more than happy to help me find a job and give me recommendations. I saw examples of people who were wonderful mothers and were able to work either part or full time. I started wondering if it would work to teach a little bit or if Seth and I could work out a schedule to tend the baby.

One winter morning, the snow was so bad that I drove Seth to school instead of making him face the drifts on a bike. After dropping him off, I drove myself home in the car. The roads were deserted, and everything was covered with a foot of fresh snow. As I crept along the snowy roads, I looked out the window at the white trees and pristine ground. I turned off the radio and let my mind wander. I started replaying a conversation from the night before with a friend who was expecting twins. I had told her that I hadn't figured out what to do about work yet. She said she felt the same way and told me that she didn't want to "just be at home." As I thought about the conversation, I said to myself, "I should just decide that I want to be home with my baby and not be ashamed to tell people. The world needs more people who are proud to be raising their children." I immediately felt a rush of the Spirit. I hadn't felt so good about anything in months. A thought came to me: "That's the best decision you've ever made." *Wait! Had I even made a decision? What about part-time jobs? Teaching night classes?* But I knew the Spirit was guiding my path. I couldn't deny the feeling that I should put my family first and not worry about finding a job. As I made that choice, I sometimes felt that I was going directly against the stream of the world, but I gained strength by reading the words of the prophets. I especially loved the words of President James E. Faust:

> If you have the choice, do not abandon too quickly the full-time career of marriage and mothering. You don't have to earn money to be important. You may choose not to sell your time. As you consider a professional career, remember that no one will love you more than those in your own home. In the business or scientific world, no one would consider you to be perfect. But your little ones, for a time, will think that you are perfect. And if you are wise, they will adore you for eternity.[7]

I knew being a full-time mother would be hard, but I felt at peace.

About a year later, again in the winter, I found myself sitting at the kitchen table next to a high chair and a screaming baby. Joseph, now seven months old, had already wiped mushed-up carrots all over the high chair tray and all over his face. He was now playing with a ladle as I tried to give him one last bite. I finally gave up on the carrots and offered him a little chunk of bread, which he grabbed, looked at, and promptly tossed on the floor. As I bent over (once again) to clean up his mess, an unexpected thought entered my mind: *I love what I do*. I sat back up, surprised, looking at my messy baby. I thought back over the last few months with Joseph—his content little fists as he nursed and fell asleep, his first laugh when we were changing his dirty diaper at the beach, his quick smile at anyone who would look at him, and his little shuffle crawl across our hardwood floors. I remembered the stress I felt in college when I was trying to pick a major but unable to focus my passion on any one field. I realized that *this* was the passion I had been looking for. I loved my child and that love, a perfect Christlike love, made me feel complete.

Although I felt confident that being at home with my son was the right thing to do, I still worried—mostly about having more children. We'd had our first child right away, but what should we do about a second? I didn't feel like being pregnant again, but I didn't feel right about doing anything to prevent it. So we didn't. Things would work out as they were supposed to. Even though it was winter (or perhaps because of it), I started anticipating all the fun we would have in the summer—biking, running, hiking, swimming. Seth and I could even train for and do a triathlon. Then at the end of the summer, after having my fill of races, lakes and boating, I would get pregnant and have a baby the next spring. It sounded perfect. I stood in our pink bathroom in front of the sink, looking in the mirror, and asked Heavenly Father if that would be okay. "Can I just have the summer, and then I'll get pregnant and have another baby?" A thought came rather quickly: "This summer is Heavenly Father's little gift to you." I smiled, excited for all of the fun we would have. Little did I know what kind of gift Heavenly Father had in mind.

One cold February morning, Seth was leaving for school. I was in a horrible mood and started crying over nothing.

"I don't know why I'm crying," I mumbled as he put on his bike helmet and came over to give me a hug.

"Are you pregnant?" Seth joked with a smile on his face. We both laughed as he headed out the door to work.

After he left, I started wondering. What if I *was* pregnant? I couldn't rid myself of my curiosity, so I went into the bedroom and scrounged up the dollar store pregnancy test my mom had sent me a year earlier. Should I take it? I decided I might as well know. I followed the instructions for the test and watched as one little blue line showed up and then another. Positive. I left the bathroom, shaking. Joseph was only eight months old. I was still nursing. What was I going to do? When Seth came home, I waited until after he had put his bike away.

"Seth, I have some big news," I said.

"What?" he asked interested.

"Well, I couldn't stop thinking about what you said this morning before you left . . ."

"Are you . . . ?"

"Pregnant." I nodded my head.

"Are pregnancy tests ever wrong?" Seth asked.

"I don't think so."

"Oh, wow," he said, sitting down on the couch and running his hands through his hair. "Wow."

I wasn't sure when I had gotten pregnant but figured the baby would probably be due around October. I went to the doctor to have an ultrasound for an estimated due date. With Joseph squirming in his car seat on the floor, I lay uncomfortably on the table, hoping this appointment would go quickly. The doctor slapped some cold gel on my stomach and began making slow circles with the ultrasound. We both were staring intently at the screen.

"Hmmmm. I'm not seeing anything that looks like a pregnancy," he said. We both jumped as a huge vertebral column, not a small mass of cells, went swimming across the screen. He zoomed the ultrasound out and there, happy as could be, was a nineteen-and-a-half-week-old baby. Instead of an October baby, we came home expecting a baby boy in July.

As the pregnancy became more real, so did my excitement. The two of them would be thirteen months apart. But then I couldn't think of anyone I knew who had babies *that* close and I started feeling strange. We hadn't told anyone yet, but we would need to soon for obvious reasons. Once again, I began worrying about what people would say. Would they think we were crazy for having kids so fast? People had been happy for us when we were having our first baby, but would it be the same with a second? What would people in Seth's lab think? What would people in the ward think?

I found my peace in the temple a few weeks after finding out I was pregnant. After the session, I walked slowly through the celestial room. As I approached the doors, I heard a sound in my mind—not a voice, or a song—but a cheer going up on the other side of the veil. Somehow I knew it was my children cheering for me. I knew that even if no one else understood what I was going through, or if no one else appreciated what I was doing, they did. At that moment, I wouldn't have cared what anyone in the world said. I felt a love for my children, present and future, surge through me. As I walked through that holy place, my perspective became clear. Small nagging thoughts and worries of what other people thought seemed miniscule in comparison with the love I felt.

I now have two children, Joseph and little Kenny. Shortly after my second son, Kenny, was born, we read 1 Nephi 8 as a family. My husband asked if there was a time when I felt like I had tasted the fruit of the tree of life. All I could think about was when I finally held Kenny for the first time. There he was, dark hair, screaming, my little son. In that moment, I felt true joy. In Lehi's vision, there are those who make it to the tree of life, taste of the fruit, but feel embarrassed by the people pointing and laughing at them, and fall away in shame. Then there are the faithful, like Lehi and Nephi, who amid the laughing and the mocking, stay true to what matters most. By choosing motherhood, I have felt the love of God; I have tasted of the fruit of the tree of life. What seemed difficult to me at first has now become my greatest blessing. Even though I know how hard it will be, I can't wait to have more children. And though people may laugh or point, mock or stare, I've learned to follow the example of Nephi and Lehi, who heard the voices "but heeded them not" (1 Nephi 8:33).

# THIS IS THE LIFE!

*by Elise Hahl*

I'm pretty sure I should be teaching sign language to my kids right now. I should be playing scripture finger puppets or teaching them to change the lint filter of the dryer, at least. But the minute I see the oversized beanbag chair in the corner of our playroom, I'm done. I plop down, nestle into my tan, leathery pouf and let the voices of my children fade.

"This is the life," I say, with a faint sigh. I don't really know sign language anyway.

A few seconds into my reverie, the thumping of little feet makes my heart start to beat faster. I try to ignore it, to pretend I'm not about to lose this paradise, but the rumble of footsteps grows closer and louder until it's almost on top of me. "AAAAHHHHH!" they scream. I see four feet, two torsos, four brown eyes. Before I know it, two boys are pouncing on my ribs, tickling my sides, and shoving me off the beanbag. Repeat.

It's a game we call "This is the Life!" in our family. Each of us takes a turn pretending to relax in the beanbag chair (or in my case, truly hoping to snooze) while the others plan an ambush. Other families teach their children to sew or sing in harmony; we do this. Even my toddler has learned to say, "Dis is da ife." And now it's becoming clear to me that I've played this game too many times because I've begun to see it as a metaphor for my own life after marriage.

It all began in a relaxing, peaceful way. I married the man who sent regular, chocolate-stuffed care packages to me when I was a missionary in Brazil. I had to or else my companions would have. Oliver and I lived abroad for our first year of marriage, first in Switzerland, then in Brazil. We spent our weekdays working and our weekends hiking in Bavaria or beach-bumming in Rio. I couldn't imagine a sweeter paradise.

Before we could clink our parasol-adorned drinks together and say, "This is the life," we saw that life, as we knew it, would change. A few months into our marriage, Oliver and I were sitting together in a room of the temple in Bern, Switzerland, when our conversation turned to children. I said something about the baby name we liked best at the time, "Caleb George." The moment the name left my lips, Caleb George felt so close that I could almost feel him sitting with Oliver and me, right there on the sofa. A few months later, we were thrilled to find out that we were indeed expecting a child—a boy.

It was during the second trimester, after we moved back to the States, that I started to wonder what on earth we had done to ourselves. I felt threatened by the future, as if I could hear the first pattering of footsteps in the distance, ready to jump on me.

I had thought I'd prepared for motherhood; I had listened to tales of widening hips and thinning sanity. Still, I found myself mourning the loss of a mobile, footloose lifestyle with Oliver as the due date drew nearer. How would we manage quick getaways to Barcelona with a pack-and-play and stroller to tote? Did having kids mean we wouldn't be able to sleep in on Saturdays for the next twenty years? And more important, how would I feel when professional doors closed on me for choosing motherhood at this age, especially if I became the involved, hands-on kind of mom I wanted to be? Most of the other twenty-five-year-olds I knew were nurturing careers, not babies: a former college roommate of mine was selling fixed-income securities on Wall Street, another was conducting marine research in Hawaii, and an old foosball buddy was about to sell his own Silicon Valley company for a gazillion dollars. I had been a class president at Stanford the year before my mission, an achiever in my own right (if you count the successful orchestration of Class Bowling Night as an achievement, which I totally do). How would I explain myself in the alumni book?

In humbler moments at church or on my own, I felt more prepared to walk away from my little Eden—a world of visible accomplishment, personal time, and easy dinners out. The love for my unborn children in those moments felt weightier than any attachment to a life I was giving up. Plus, by that time, the decision had already been made. The footsteps were nearly on top of me.

Soon Caleb George joined our family, and then his little brother, Chase, did too. They amazed and enchanted us. They also rammed us out of the snug little beanbag of a life we had created. Caleb and Chase taught me hard truths: Sometimes work-life balance meant holding a crying infant on my lap while teaching a piano lesson. Fashion meant embracing the maternity overalls, not fearing them. And motherhood in general meant that I was so important that I couldn't make a trip to the bathroom without hearing a protest from at least one family member.

A few years later, the challenges of parenting still surprise me at times. It never occurs to me that these are the richest years of my life when I'm schlepping two shrieking boys and a month's worth of toilet paper up the stairs after a trip to the supermarket. I never wax poetic about maternal responsibility when it involves waking up five times a night to help my four-year-old put on his blanket, take off his blanket, chase away a nightmare, drink a little cup of water, and then change a full set of wet sheets.

But even though I might daydream about a neater, prettier family life sometimes, I know that raising children has to be this hard. It wouldn't be rewarding, or even real, if my every waking moment were material for a parenting magazine ad. It wouldn't force me to grow. And it wouldn't teach me the price—and joy—of caring for another human being.

My younger son, Chase, taught me something about the value of struggling, although at first I never dreamed that he would. Large and round from birth, he fell asleep easily at night. He stayed quiet in the morning, ready to beam at us the minute we walked through the door. He ate hearty portions of oatmeal without protesting, unlike his brother (and father). He loved to hold his cheek next to mine, and he could cuddle with me for an entire church service without squirming. He was all dessert, no calories.

By ten months, Chase had mastered a crawl that made

his rump zigzag with every movement. I found it so charming that I made his crawl the subject of an essay for a writing class in my master's program. I didn't want him to ever grow out of it. By the time he reached his first birthday, he hadn't. Thirteen months came along and he was still crawling. Then fourteen. My husband and I weren't worried because we assumed he would walk by fifteen months, the tail end of the normal range. Fifteen months came and went. I entered "late walker" into a search engine on my laptop and found good news—babies like Chase were actually smarter than the ones who were already walking! But when I brought him to the pediatrician for a routine appointment, the doctor took a long look at him.

"Hold him up to a standing position, and then let go," she commanded. I propped him up and released my hands. Immediately, he collapsed into a cute little heap.

The doctor wasn't amused. "If he's not walking by eighteen months," she said, "we'll have to bring him in for neurological tests." She recommended that we find a physical therapist immediately.

I struggled to speak as she jotted down a few phone numbers for me, but I couldn't say anything. The poster of the food pyramid on the wall grew blurry. Therapy? Neurological tests? Was something really wrong with him? How could I have missed this?

On the way home from the doctor's office, I arranged for physical therapy on my cell phone. A few weeks later, two unsmiling women came to our house and scribbled on clipboards for a half hour while Chase sat. They tried to get him to stand, to crawl, anything—but really, they scared the sweatpants off of him. Their official report concluded that Chase had the gross motor skills of a child a little more than half his age. If I hadn't already seen children seven months younger toddle circles around Chase, I might not have believed it.

My husband and I began praying that he would walk. We bought him a pricey pair of navy blue, yellow-striped sneakers, in the hopes that the shoes' much-lauded "motion system" would jumpstart his career as a walker. We brought Chase to parks where he could practice walking on a rougher surface, and used puzzle pieces and walker toys to entice him. But still, whenever he lost support, he would crumple to the ground.

Over the next couple of months, people still thought Chase was textbook adorable, but they grew quiet when I told them how old he was. Even the UPS man was concerned. "He's not walking yet?" he asked. Friends of a more laissez-faire persuasion (bless them) would say, "Every child starts walking when they're ready. No need to push them." But as Chase passed sixteen and then seventeen months without walking, some of them started to worry too. "Is he doing okay?" they'd ask gingerly.

We were flirting with eighteen months, and Chase was clinging to familiar things, like his green fuzzy blanket and his mommy's arms. At twenty-five pounds, he was growing harder for me to carry. When I set him on his feet, he usually slumped to his knees and crawled away, stubbornly. He had figured out a way to stay forever in his own secure, little Eden—a world where he'd never fall because he wouldn't walk. No matter how hard we tried, my husband and I couldn't force him to leave it.

The night before Chase turned eighteen months old, I started wondering whether he would survive our ward's nursery. Crawling on his hands and knees, would he be trampled by a stomping toddler? Would the leaders know how to handle him? I groaned inside as I thought about an uglier prospect—the idea of putting my son through a long series of neurological tests, now that the doctor's deadline was upon us.

I was helping Caleb into his pajamas that night when I heard my husband's voice coming from the family room. "'Lise, come quick!" he called.

I ran to the doorway. "What is it?"

"Shhh . . ." he said. And there was Chase, standing upright in the middle of the brown rug. Walking. "Sik, Seben, Eight," Chase counted, as he stepped forward toward the television. I stood there, mouth agape, as he moved ahead. "Nine, ten, eleben . . ." Chase continued. He paused at twelve, turned, and walked back toward us. We held our breaths. "Fourteen, sixteen, sebenteen . . ." Chase collapsed with a mischievous grin on his face somewhere around "twenty."

We screamed and clapped. He had done it! Scratch the neurological tests! We were too busy cheering to feel silly for ever worrying.

A few days after the breakthrough, I took the boys to a park close to home. It was one of those rare November days that had everyone back in summer clothes. We picnicked in a shady playground next to a basketball court and then walked onto an empty field, away from the swinging and sliding. The unfiltered sunlight made us squint.

Chase clutched my fingers as we navigated the ups and down in the grass, bumps that could only seem big to little shoes like his. When we reached the middle of the field, I let go of his hands. He took a few unsure little steps as he wondered how to use his new skill on this terrain, and then he took off, erupting with laughter.

Caleb and I ran around, pretending to chase Chase. He flailed his arms and squealed, tottering off in all directions. His blond mop of hair flopped around on his forehead and his cheeks grew pink. It was his first time walking outside, I realized, and he hadn't seemed so delighted in months. I could imagine him thinking, "I've watched you do this for so long and now I can finally do it!"

Of course, none of the adults at the picnic tables or swing sets had any idea that those little steps were noteworthy. I'm sure I wouldn't have seen anything extraordinary in a little boy walking if it weren't for our struggle. But there on the field, I couldn't think of a sweeter miracle than the one I was witnessing. My son had finally abandoned his comforts in pursuit of something greater, and I could hardly contain my pride.

I had left my own cozy phase of life too, somewhere in the middle of trials like this one that altered my expectations and sense of control. And even though I wouldn't mind revisiting my earlier, cushy paradise for a day or two to catch my breath, I've decided that Eden's not a place I'd like to stay. My family doesn't live there. I think I've always needed them as much as they need me. So I'm setting my permanent address in this new life—the one that lets me watch my children grow, that brings me closer to the person I want to be. It's the life that makes me struggle and scramble, but it leaves me with a bigger heart.

For me, this is the life. It's the only one I want.

# CHOOSING MOTHERHOOD

*by Emily Streeter*

If work called for an extra person, I wasn't going to answer. I wasn't going to think about tomorrow's scheduled shift, and I especially wasn't going to wonder how long it would be before I enjoyed a moment like this again. Instead, I was going to get lost with my daughter in a blizzard of bubbles. One rested on the cement, a fleeting sphere of soap that looked like a glass marble. Another floated toward my daughter. "Mommy, I catch it!" exclaimed Audrey, dimples punctuating her wide smile. Her eyes shone with excitement as she held her tiny finger up to show the prize. A mini bubble had somehow stayed strong enough to land without bursting on the tip of her outstretched hand. "Oh, you did! You caught it, Audrey!" The warmth of the Arizona sun caressed my shoulders as I took a deep breath and blew a few hundred more bubbles.

It was the kind of moment that made me ache for more—a moment that allowed me to focus solely on Audrey. I've noticed that when I push the laundry aside, let the dishes rest where they are, and allow the answering machine to take the hospital's call, my reward is a million tiny moments of joy, like those bubbles shimmering around us on a spring morning. When I allow Audrey to take me from my own world of responsibilities or selfish pursuits, I enter the world of a twenty-two-month-old, where I am rewarded with wonder, beauty, and excitement.

I had imagined, when I first became a mother, that motherhood would always be like this: me, focusing my full attention on my children, undistracted by outside responsibilities. My husband and I expected that after he finished school, and nothing would keep us from settling into the roles we had decided upon: Geoff would earn a comfortable income for our burgeoning family, and I would happily make our house into a home. I would work three days a month in order to keep my nursing license current, in case of emergency. But this dream, which seemed so sturdy when we contemplated it, has turned out to be more tenuous than we imagined. Time after graduation has not gone as planned.

Geoff graduated from Yale in December of 2009. After much prayer and consideration, we decided to move back to Arizona, where we would be close to my family. Geoff would look for work as a physician's assistant, and I would take a temporary position at the hospital I had worked in for many years prior to moving to Connecticut. After my husband found a job, I would cut back on my hours and focus my attention on our daughter.

The first challenge to our resolve for me to stay home came quickly. Just one day into the first week back at work, I received word that my old management position was opening again. I was approached by the assistant director and asked to consider the position. Many of my coworkers encouraged me to return to my previous responsibility. I wished in some ways that I *could* do it again. I had loved that position. After five years of nursing, I had found myself sitting in counsel with the leaders of the organization, helping to make decisions that affected the entire hospital. I had developed classes, mentored new nurses, and challenged experienced nurses to teach younger nurses. I loved the work, the hours, and the interaction I had with the people. The wages and opportunities for advancement were attractive too.

Still, the position was full time and sometimes required more than a forty-hour work week to fulfill its responsibilities. So to each person, I made the same reply: "I've chosen to work only a little. While we were gone, I became a mother and my priority right now is my daughter."

The second test has come inch by inch—a much more grueling exercise in learning. It has come despite our best efforts to push it or pray it away. For now, it is six months past graduation and Geoff hasn't started working yet. He has struggled to find a local position as a PA. Of necessity, I have once again delved into nursing on a full-time basis. And at first, I loved it.

Bedside nursing is different than the management position I turned down, but it has its own challenges and rewards. When I can make a patient who is nervous about an upcoming procedure laugh, I am happy too. Figuring out something crucial to the patient's health that the doctor may not have seen is an exercise in critical thinking that I enjoy. Floor nursing can be physically demanding work, and that gives me a feeling of satisfaction at the end of the day. At work I know what is expected of me during the day and there is a preset schedule to keep—unlike motherhood! Working with colleagues who are good-natured is also a plus.

But even as I feel the happiness that comes from nursing, sadness and a discontent is growing. "Bubble" moments with Audrey have become too few and far between. I don't have time to do all the things I used to do when I was not working full time. I am not recording events in a journal, and I rarely take pictures. I miss making homemade bread and trying new recipes. We have not formed friendships with others in our neighborhood because I am so often unavailable.

But my internal conflict is not just because of the things I cannot do with Audrey. Part of me is growing frustrated because I am limited in my nursing abilities as well. Prior to becoming a mother, I could spend time growing in nursing. I could take on new challenges, like familiarizing myself with all the responsibilities required in the intensive care unit. But now that I have more than just work, I do not have the energy to devote to expanding my skills and knowledge. Now I struggle with feeling that I am doing many things, none of them as well as I'd like.

Soon, Geoff will begin working, and I will not have to work full time. Once again, I will choose how to devote my energy and time. But I already know what I will choose: I will be a mother. I may never have any worldly reward to show for my efforts on any given day. I will have added responsibilities without a promotion, extra-long hours without a bonus, and monotonous tasks that will be mine alone to perform.

But many moments and people have prepared me to

choose motherhood as a priority. I have compelling reasons for becoming a mother and choosing to do it full-time.

First, I have decided to dedicate myself to being a mother because I grew up listening to prophets and apostles encouraging mothers to be as involved as possible at home. I remember the feelings I had as I listened to leaders teach of the importance of motherhood. I recall the themes of the talks on motherhood and how they impressed on my mind the significance of this role. For example, on numerous occasions President Spencer W. Kimball urged mothers to "come home . . . to your children, born and unborn. Wrap the motherly cloak about you and, *unembarrassed,* help in a major role to create the bodies for the immortal souls who anxiously wait."[8]

The words of the prophets also helped as I shaped an opinion of what being a victorious woman entails. President David O. McKay taught, "she who rears successfully a family of healthy, beautiful sons and daughters, whose influence will be felt through generations to come . . . deserves the highest honor that man can give, and the choicest blessings of God."[9]

As I pondered the principle of choosing motherhood as a "career" back when I was first married, I remember going on a long walk one day on the trails that lace through the greenbelts of our neighborhood. I was preparing to teach a lesson to the sixteen- and seventeen-year-olds about the importance of motherhood. As the wind rustled the leaves overhead, the exercise and the solitude helped me think about my life and what my roles would be. Why is motherhood important? Why be educated to just stay home and care for crying babies?

As I walked, I remembered a recent conversation with my husband. I had been talking with him about the transition from nursing to being a mother. "It is going to be a big transition for me to be a stay-at-home mom. What if I don't like it? What if I'm bored to tears?" I had asked. I knew I had a testimony of motherhood, but I was afraid. Working as a nurse had brought feelings of competence and contribution. What if I was not cut out for this sort of work and I failed? What if I did not find as much meaning in being a stay-at-home mom? Would others see me as less successful or significant?

As I walked, I had a moment of realization that still gives meaning to my work of mothering. If I worked all my life as a nurse, I would be one person helping society. If, however, I dedicated myself to raising *six* children to be contributing, honorable members of society, then six people would contribute followed by their children and grandchildren to follow. My influence for good, therefore, would be exponentially greater when channeled into the work of mothering.

I have learned by living other principles of the restored gospel that obedience to God's direction brings peace and joy. I know, therefore, that I can take comfort in His counsel. Among his very first commandments was the mandate, "Be fruitful, and multiply" (Genesis 1:22). He teaches that my most important work is motherhood; that it will bring the most joy. I trust that it is so. And I know that He will help me.

Second, I will devote my time to mothering because I have found that I cannot do both full-time nursing and motherhood with as much passion and energy as I can devote to one alone.

During the October 2007 general conference, Sister

Julie B. Beck encouraged women to choose to do less so that there is more time to do the work of mothering. She said, "Mothers who know are willing to live on less and consume less of the world's goods in order to spend more time with their children—more time eating together, more time working together, more time reading together, more time talking, laughing, singing, and exemplifying. These mothers choose carefully and do not try to choose it all. . . . That is influence; that is power."[10]

I continue to gain strength and direction from the living apostles. Several General Authorities during the April 2010 general conference gave talks encouraging excellence in the work of mothering. Elder L. Tom Perry reminded that fathers are primarily responsible to provide the necessities of life while mothers are primarily responsible for the nurture of their children. He continues, "In these sacred responsibilities, fathers and mothers are obligated to help one another as equal partners. . . . While circumstances do vary and the ideal isn't always possible, I believe it is by divine design that the role of motherhood emphasizes the nurturing and teaching of the next generation."[11]

I have received firsthand confirmation over the past six months that this principle is inspired. I feel blessed that during this time I have been able to step up as an equal partner to share in providing for our family while it has been necessary. However, when I drag myself home after thirteen hours at the hospital, I feel relief that in time, I will not be expected to excel at both providing for my family and nurturing my children. I am increasingly grateful that there is a division of labor. I feel thankful when I come home to folded laundry, scrubbed floors, and stories of how Audrey spent quality time with her daddy. Working has also given me a deep appreciation for the intense labor my husband is willing to undertake when he begins working. I am more considerate of what a blessing it will be to have someone who is willing and able to take the lion's share of that burden as his responsibility.

I am also more keenly aware of the many women whose circumstances are such that they do not have the choice to be at home with their children. Life would be so neat and tidy if everything always went as expected. But spouses become disabled, lose their jobs, leave their families, or even die young. I know women in each of these circumstances and can empathize a little more because of my current situation. This time where it has been necessary for me to work has strengthened my desire to be a good mother, not lessened it. I feel the yearnings of a mother who still has deep love and every good desire for her children but less time and energy readily available to spend. I have learned that women who are mothers and full-time providers need to be supported, encouraged, and championed as they strive to fill two important roles. This knowledge can help me support others better in the future.

Third, I want to be a successful mother, which will require that I make it my focus, instead of thinking of motherhood as a distraction from other "more important" things. Making it my quest will require a great deal of my strength.

Before I had Audrey, I remember telling others, "Once I'm not working full time, I'll have more time for this or that." Ha! That shows just how blissfully ignorant I was about the work it takes to be a mother. The first few months of sleepless nights and long days of soothing my crying, colicky child taught me that mothering definitely qualifies as work. Toddlerhood has brought different, but no less demanding challenges. Potty training? Leadership over a hospital committee would be much easier!

In reality, I find that being the sort of mother and wife I want to be takes patience, organization, creativity, and endurance. Some of my past experiences have helped prepare me for this work. My mission in the Philippines helped me to be less shy, more courageous, and better at making friends. Now I count this talent as important so that Audrey grows up socializing with good people. Playing with other kids brings her as much joy as true friendship brings to me.

My years at BYU helped me understand how to study and learn. I spent many long hours in the library, striving to prepare to care for sick people. Even in my college years, though, I never had as much thirst for knowledge as I do now, grappling with child-rearing problems (sleep habits, tantrums, developing independence, and so on). I scour books, the Internet, and scriptures, searching for answers. I am motivated because I know that I am working to build a healthy, well-adapted human being.

My experience as a bedside nurse has taught me patience, organization, and planning to guide healing and the advancement of health. Many times as a nurse I've prayed for added strength and inspiration and it has come. As a manager I learned motivational skills and developed more loving leadership.

Yet all these experiences and qualities I thought I had

developed are challenged anew as I take on the tasks of a mother. I am learning more patience, more diligence, more creativity, more need for love, and more perseverance than I have through any other experience thus far.

Every success in my life so far has come by the grace of a loving Heavenly Father. In every instance, he has asked that I devote all the energy and focus I can muster. And so, as I undertake motherhood, I do not want to do it with partial devotion. I do not want to look back with regret and see that I have failed because I could not decide to make it my first and foremost priority.

Finally, I choose motherhood because I truly want to. My best memories and deepest joys continue to come from relationships, particularly those with my family.

I loved hiking as a young girl, sitting with my mother at the piano, learning algebra from my dad, giggling with my sisters into the wee hours of the night, snowboarding with my brothers, and listening to my grandpa's life stories. When I picture Christmas Eve with its lights, music, scripture, and family, warmth envelops me. As a mother, I want Audrey and any children yet to come to have the opportunity to grow in a positive learning environment. Ultimately, my job is to create the kind of home that fosters joyful moments and cultivates character as we all strive together to follow the example of our Savior, Jesus Christ.

My hope for Audrey is that she will grow into a woman worthy of her name, which means "noble strength." It is a derivative of her maternal grandmother's name, who was a mother of six and a woman of heroic integrity, humor, love, and service.

I know that in order to ensure happy memories for my daughter, I have to work hard in the present to support the joy of family. Just like any pursuit in which I want to succeed, making a greater effort, I have learned, will lead to greater, sweeter rewards. What are some of the rewards I have already experienced as a result of choosing motherhood? The returns for my labor as a mother have often surpassed my expectations. How can I describe the joy I feel when Audrey takes my face with her tiny hands, draws me close, and plants a kiss on my cheek? Or the way her laughter warms my heart when she marches around the room or leaps from the footrest to the couch? What sweeter music is there than the first-uttered phrases such as, "Let's make a fruit smoozie" or her first solo of *Twinkle, Twinkle, Little Star*? How can I help but get excited about the day when my two-year-old lists the possibilities?—"Mom, tomorrow we can go to the park, swim at the pool, make a treat, stop by Grandma and Grandpa's, and buy peas and blananas at the store!" What sweeter reminder of the importance of people could there be than the early prayers of our little one, who made a habit of listing all the dozens of people she loves by name? No requests. Just gratitude for those she is closest to.

When Audrey was just seven months old, one of her favorite things to do was walk around the room. She couldn't walk on her own yet but did very well if I held both of her hands tightly and came with her. Now she walks and even runs without my help, but when she needs to cross the street, I clasp one hand tightly in mine and we do it together. Too soon, she will not need or want me to hold her hand. But I will walk beside her and continue to love and guide her. And far too fast after that, she will drive off to college to pursue a life of her own. But I will write her. And when the phone rings, I will answer and listen as she shares her experiences and asks for my advice. Like the fleeting bubble that rested on her finger, the time when she needs me for a large part of the day will be gone. But I will be left with memories of the time that was given me, and I will have a daughter who has become a woman who I hope will enjoy a cherished, dear friendship with me, just as I do with my mother. And I will be left with the greatest reward of all: I will always be Audrey's mother.

# MAKING A DIFFERENCE

*by Lia Collings*

My husband was graduating, but all eyes were on the red-sequined beauty at his side. "Justin Michael Collings," the announcer read deliberately, "and Little Collings," she added, noting the flitting four-year-old next to him. The sun flashed off "Little's" smile and sequins alike as she skipped across the stage alongside her daddy, both hands clasping his. Justin took his diploma, walked down the ramp, and returned our daughter to me, where I waited with two more red-sequined little girls. I guided my children back to a secluded area of the Gothic courtyard to resume our game of Duck, Duck, Goose until the ceremonies concluded; Justin slipped back into his seat with the other graduates.

That was it. If someone had told me, years ago, how insignificant watching my husband graduate from the Yale Law School would be, I would have raised a disbelieving eyebrow. My, how seven years have altered us.

Justin and I entered our marriage determined to change the world. We spent our honeymoon strategizing what degrees, schools, and career paths would make our dreams of a modern golden age come true. He would attend the best law school he could get into, and I would attend law school at BYU while he finished his undergraduate degree. A good speaker but a bad politician, he would make some friends and get a government appointment. I would study anything and everything in the law related to education and eventually cure our nation of educational underperformance and inequality. I was then a BYU senior majoring in classics, and four years in the company of the greatest statesmen and poets of ancient Greece and Rome had filled me with a sense of public spirit and a desire to change the world. Our course was mapped.

Nine months later, just in time for graduation, Julia Madison arrived on the scene. We prepared ourselves to iron out a few wrinkles but kept the basic plan laid out on the table. Justin registered for whatever classes would accommodate my schedule as I began a master's in public policy with an emphasis on education, since the timing of law school wouldn't work out for me. I even mapped out the mothers' lounges closest to my classes. We were set . . . we thought.

One day early in the semester, I stayed a few minutes after class to discuss a paper with my professor. Glancing at my watch as I darted out the door, I wondered how loud my child's howls of hunger would be. Long before I reached our meeting spot in front of the Harold B. Lee Library, I heard unmistakable newborn shrieks echoing off the glass walls of the atrium. I broke into a run, my backpack awkwardly pounding against my body, and without a pause grabbed my baby from my husband's outstretched arms. I knew he was calling out the particulars of my offenses as I pushed through the doors and beelined for the nearest mothers' lounge, but Julia's cries drowned out everything but his irritated tone.

Haphazardly settled on the rough, brown couch, Julia sought solace in food as I tried to calm my own nerves and racing heart. "You're okay," I said soothingly, as much to myself as to her. "You're okay, you're okay." We couldn't have been sitting for more than thirty seconds before lights started flashing and deafening sirens began to blare. Fire alarm. Perfect. I contemplated hiding out and finishing the feeding, but the piercing sirens had set Julia screaming and flailing anyway. I gathered my baggage and ran up the stairs, clutching a diaper bag, backpack, and famished child. When we finally resumed our feeding a full thirty minutes later, I tried to tell myself things would get better.

They didn't. By four weeks I had begun to resent my daughter. I saw calm, happy babies in every lap but mine. I heard talk of other babies taking two-hour naps multiple times a day and wondered what doctor I could get to prescribe that drug for *my* child. Julia didn't exactly fit the bill for "colicky," but I seemed to spend all my time trying to silence her. Digging a little deeper I wondered if Julia never smiled or laughed because she rarely saw me do so. Perhaps her lack of calm reflected my own.

Domestic tranquility wasn't the only thing suffering; Justin and I were both pulling the worst grades of our lives. I began to look at cold hard facts: no one could get into Harvard Law with a 3.0 GPA, and the Department of Education probably didn't hire folks who slinked through a master's program at BYU. I could stubbornly—and selfishly—pursue my degree to the end, at the expense of everyone and everything that mattered to me, or I could defer my goals for the sake of *ours*.

Six long weeks into the semester, I unilaterally decided to withdraw. I remember walking from the administration building to the Kimball tower to meet Justin for the usual trade-off. My spirits matched the bright September sunshine. "Where's your backpack?" he asked, as I walked slowly toward him, smiling behind the stroller. He had seen neither slowness nor smiles from me of late. "What's going on?" he asked in confusion. I hesitated, not knowing exactly how he'd take the news. "I dropped out," I said, handing him the yellow transaction receipt. "I withdrew from my program." He stared at me, uncomprehending. He knew I wanted to make a real difference in the world; he knew I had had an eye on education reform for as long as he had known me; he knew this was a sizable sacrifice for me, and that I had made it for him and our family. When the full meaning of this action finally registered, his hazel eyes shone with gratitude and his shoulders seemed to relax as though a heavy weight had fallen from them.

I felt the same way—for the first few days. But when the novelty of full-time motherhood wore off, the disappointment of frustrated ambition set in. All my life I had dreamed of doing something extraordinary. For years I had planned on employing my unique training and perspective to improve the lives of thousands. I would make a difference; I would *be* different. But now I spent my time doing exactly what every other woman my age seemed to be doing—mothering a young child. I still worked part time from home on a project I found very meaningful and supplemented that with small outside endeavors that—I thought—did something that really *mattered.* But still, though I knew in my heart I had done the right thing, the loss felt very real.

Things were going decidedly better for my husband. Associations he formed that fateful semester, together with rigorous study for the LSAT, led to admittance at every law school to which he applied. On a snowy day in early December, he received acceptance calls from Harvard and Stanford within an hour of each other. We were obviously thrilled. Yale had been his top choice because of its storied tradition of producing academics and statesmen. But we were more than happy to "settle" for Harvard and planned to move to Cambridge the next fall. Late in the admissions period, however, the call from Yale finally came. We immediately set our course for New Haven. We were so sure that Yale was the right choice that Justin didn't even attend new student weekend. Our second daughter, Elisabeth, threatened to arrive that weekend anyway. We were sitting on top of the world.

The euphoria lasted about four months. From birth, Elisabeth had an unusually large head. My husband's relatives assured me it was genetic—"Why, Grandpa Ralph had to stretch his hats out on a watermelon! It's because of all those brains!"—but I wasn't so sure. I measured her head circumference weekly and searched the Internet for any clues to its cause, but other than a large forehead, she had no worrisome symptoms. I tried to tell myself it was nothing.

Ten days after we arrived in New Haven I could quiet the nagging no longer. "We have *got* to go to the doctor," I announced.

"It's Saturday," Justin said.

"Their urgent care is open."

"Our car's dead and it's raining," he noted.

"It's only a mile. We can walk."

"If it *is* something serious, our Yale insurance doesn't start until classes do," he countered, thinking a reference to our paper-thin pocketbook would surely win the day.

"There is something *wrong*!" I insisted. "I'm going by myself if you're not coming."

A walk in the rain later, our fears were confirmed. "You need to go to the emergency room," the white-mustached doctor said firmly. "Now." We called a new friend in the ward to secure a ride to the hospital for me and Eli. The drive seemed interminable, and Anna, bless her soul, listened through the whole of it as I shared my fears about Eli. Our friends back in Utah had a little boy with a large forehead, I told her. Doctors had discovered a tumor, operated on it, and placed a shunt. Four months after diagnosis their little boy was gone. Anna tried to find a bright side.

We finally arrived at the hospital and Anna waited with me, unasked, through hours of procedures. The doctors performed CT scans and MRIs to determine the cause of Eli's large head. Doctors, residents, and medical students asked me the same list of questions time and again, the answers to most of which were "No." "Then how did you know anything was wrong?" they'd finally ask. "I've been watching her," I said simply. The doctors were baffled. "You must be a very observant mother," they told me.

Doctors finally came back with news: there was no tumor. Eli was suffering from hydrocephalus, commonly called "water on the brain," but her condition came about because one passageway in the middle of her brain was too narrow to allow all the brain fluid to pass. Even without the tumor, the excess fluid enlarged her head and put pressure on her brain, a circumstance that would lead to brain damage and death if left unchecked. They recommended the placement of a shunt, a little plastic tube running from the empty spaces inside her brain down into her abdomen. A well-placed shunt would divert excess fluid to a place where her body could absorb it, they explained. We booked ourselves a room in the hospital for the night.

The Lord showered His tender mercies upon me from the beginning. The resident who had taken our case in the emergency room was one Mark Cicero—a reassuring echo of my favorite Roman author, Marcus Tullius Cicero. Years before, Cicero had inspired me with his eloquent calls to fortitude, virtue, and courage under fire. The Lord blessed us to find help too, even in a city 2,300 miles from home that we'd lived in for ten days. When Justin wondered aloud who could help him administer to Eli before surgery, I immediately volunteered a friend from high school who happened to be working at Yale. Other than my husband and my father, there was no other man whose worthiness before the Lord I trusted more. This man's wonderful wife then rallied the ward to our cause. In addition to prayers and fasting, ward members provided meals, babysitting, cleaning, and even CDs for our hospital room.

The surgery, by all accounts, went well. We were back home the following Wednesday, just in time for Justin to begin classes. This obviously hadn't been an ideal prologue to our law school years, but this fiery ordeal had at least helped us forge a strong bond with our new ward. Already we rejoiced in the wonderful associations that would deepen over the next three years and pledged ourselves to repay the selfless service our ward had rendered us. We prepared ourselves for the long haul of putting the man of the house through law school, grateful that Eli was okay and that things could now get back to normal.

Within five days we were back in the hospital. The shunt had become infected, and, as often happens, the treatment was worse than the illness. I watched, helpless, as hospital staff conducted veritable torture sessions on my five-month-old baby—blowing every vein in her little arms in a series of failed efforts to place IVs, tapping the shunt with foot-long needles, externalizing the shunt so that her brain fluid drained into a little bottle next to her head, forbidding her to eat lest the neurosurgery team feel the urge to operate, unannounced. The staff of the Yale-New Haven hospital might have made effective interrogators during the Holy Inquisition.

I did what I could for Eli, though it felt like very little. She had never learned to drink from a bottle, so I lay next to her in her hospital bed so she could nurse. I sat by her side and read to myself while she slept; I played classical CDs and read to her when she awoke. I held her when that was allowed and stroked her arms and baby hands when it wasn't. Eli underwent four surgeries over the course of our stay as neurosurgeons tried to determine the location and extent of the infection.

At home, of course, things were floundering. Julia bounced from ward member to ward member when Justin went to class. Having our firstborn spend entire days with strangers only added to our stress. My mom finally flew out to care for Julia and attend to our apartment, trying her best to fill in for me at home. Still, I had it on good authority that her pancakes were nothing like mine, and she didn't do the right actions for *Guess How Much I Love You.*

After twenty aching days of uncertainty, the infection finally began to clear. We were released with powerful antibiotics and strict instructions on how to administer them, but we were home! The day after our homecoming I set to work baking bread, doing laundry, and cleaning up after my potty-training two-year-old—all the ordinary things I had missed so much during the last three weeks.

We hoped things would soon get back to normal, but over the next couple weeks, Eli often woke up screaming at night, and her shunt track seemed to be getting larger rather than smaller. I called the neurosurgery physician's assistant more than once to express my concern. She assured me that Eli's screaming was just her way of adjusting to life back at home; as for the shunt track, it would take some time for the swelling to go down.

We did our best to adjust to Eli's new challenges. Justin outlined ambitious study schedules so he could catch up with his classes; I started looking at the undergraduate course schedule for classes I might like to audit the following semester. After a few weeks back at home, a friend in the ward who sang with the Metropolitan Opera offered us a complimentary set of orchestra-seat tickets to a show she was performing in that weekend. Justin and I discussed whether we could go, ultimately deciding that Eli's nighttime difficulties prevented our leaving her to the care of a babysitter. "Same old story," I said. "Drudgery and boredom on account of my children."

I got my excitement. The night of the missed show, Eli screamed almost nonstop. After she began dry-heaving, I called the doctor. A familiar order followed: "Get to the emergency room. Now." Neurosurgeons discovered that the shunt had ripped out of place leaving "impressive" amounts of blood in her brain and causing a shunt malfunction.

I sat conscience-stricken at her crib-side in the intensive care unit. Why could I not just content myself with being a mom? Worse, why could I not do a decent job of it? I had known something was wrong with Eli. I had called and told the doctors something was wrong. It had been obvious that what I was seeing was not normal, but I thought—mistakenly—that Eli's doctors must know more than I did and hadn't pushed the issue. Why had I not trusted that I was entitled to revelation regarding her? Cerebral bleeding and shunt malfunctions posed a very real threat of serious brain damage. Would God punish my baby for *my* faults? "I'm sorry, I'm sorry, I'm sorry!" I prayed. "*Please* protect her! *Please heal her!*"

We came home from the hospital five days later, after the doctors readjusted the shunt, but in my despair, I concluded that my sins of discontent stained too red to be washed away easily. I remember borrowing a book from one of the nurses. "I'll return it when we're readmitted in a few weeks," I had said.

I watched Eli constantly for signs of infection, malfunction, or mental handicap. A few days before our post-operation check-up, it looked to me that the shunt had moved out of position. I pointed it out to Justin, but he assured me that was certainly impossible. Eli was keeping down her food and was maintaining a normal regimen of awaking three times a night, so there was no symptomatic indication that anything was wrong. This time, I wouldn't back down.

The checkup was scheduled for 8:00 a.m. At 6:30 that morning, I stood in the grocery store checkout line, watching through tear-filled eyes as a Muslim girl in a white scarf loaded frozen food into my cart. Justin could handle chicken nuggets and frozen pizza while we were gone. With the freezer stocked, I packed a hospital bag through my sobs and cried myself dry by the time we arrived at our appointment.

"I can't do this again," I told Justin as we drove. "*She* can't do this again. If she's 'appointed unto death' she may as well die near family. We can't bury her out here anyway."

"Honey!" Justin interrupted. "You don't even know that anything's wrong! She's acting fine."

I looked at him blankly. "We'll know within the hour," I said.

Arrived at the hospital, we followed a resident into the examination room. I told him that the shunt had slipped out of place and began detailing how I thought it had happened. He couldn't mask his amusement. Assuring me that shunts couldn't slip out of place, he walked over and began feeling Eli's head. His eyes widened as his disbelief turned to slight alarm. "You're right," he admitted. "The shunt has somehow migrated down into her neck." He looked at me and left. I felt no sense of triumph or vindication. I felt beaten and broken.

When the resident returned he came back with a man we had been longing to see. Ever since Eli's diagnosis, we had been hearing about a mysterious "Dr. Duncan," a sort of miracle-working legend of children's brain surgery. Yet through all the hospitalizations, all the surgeries, we had never even seen him. Now, finally, there stood before us not just the reputation but the man himself. A glimmer of light shone down into my pit of despair.

"Now tell me what we have here," Dr. Duncan invited in his gentle, Southern accent. He limped slightly as he approached to examine Eli, reminding me he had been convalescing from health problems of his own. He gently felt Eli's head and neck, talking to her reassuringly as he did so. Somewhere in all the talk about Dr. Duncan, I had heard he was the father of five himself, which perhaps explained his remarkable way with children. I told him the shunt had fallen out. He admitted quietly that it had. I recounted the months of difficulties we'd experienced, pointing out that if the smart guys of neurosurgery were such mess-ups, where did he expect us to turn? He listened sympathetically from a stool in the corner. After a characteristic Southern pause to be sure I had finished, he replied with simple confidence, "But now it's my turn." His faith restored mine. "Why don't you go sit in the waiting room while I get you checked in," he said kindly.

I don't know whether my harangue had cowed Dr. Duncan or whether he was just being fatherly, but he took good care of us. He held Eli as though she were his own granddaughter, he cancelled unnecessary blood draws ("She was here two weeks ago! We know her blood type!"), he dropped in a few times during our stay just to see how we were doing, he took the trouble to ask about our lives outside the hospital. Compared with the other surgeons we had dealt with, Dr. Duncan was like a cool rain after a blazing forest fire.

More important, his operation worked. Eli ate with no

problems after this surgery, already a change from her previous recoveries. She was so happy and alert that we were allowed to go home the next day.

We had been told that the first six months following a shunt placement are the most precarious—that if Eli could make it through six months without mishap, the shunt would likely last for years. The magical six months came and went. With the help of therapists Eli learned to walk; with no help from therapists she learned to talk. Anyone seeing or hearing Eli today would be hard pressed to find marks of her medical history. As we have frequently said in summarizing Eli's miraculous recovery, "All praise to the Lord and all thanks to Dr. Duncan."

A year or so after these events, a close friend berated me for wasting my education and talents on "just being a mom." She yipped about how much more I could be doing for my community and the world than "hiding my light" under two little girls in a tiny New Haven apartment. "What a waste," she said. "What a tragic waste."

That night I cried angry tears. My thoughts turned to Eli and that nightmare season of repeated surgeries and extended hospitalizations. I thought how different her outcome had been from those of other children the doctors and pamphlets described. All praise going to the Lord, I wondered if my mere presence had helped her recovery. I thought of President Harold B. Lee's counsel for mothers to "stay at the crossroads of the home."[12] Be there when the children come and go, he promised, and that will make the difference. I had stood at the crossroads every time Eli came from sleep or surgery during those harrowing four months. I had made her my primary interest. I had willingly—and not so willingly—sacrificed other worthwhile endeavors for the good of my child. I had certainly made mistakes—impressive ones—but the Lord had made up the difference.

I saw clearly that my friend was wrong. Maybe I wasn't making the differences in the world that she wanted or even that I had anticipated, but I *was* making a difference. Furthermore, even if that difference was only in the life of one little girl, that little girl mattered. But it wasn't just one little girl, it was two, and a husband to boot. Even if I only kept the bodies of those three people in good working order, that was an accomplishment. Fortunately, meals, laundry, and diaper changes constituted the smallest part of my sphere of influence. I had the gospel to teach my children. I had a home to make pleasant and welcoming for them. I had wonderful books to read to them. I had beautiful music to sing and listen and play with them. I had a whole beautiful world to rejoice in and explore with them. I could make *quite* a difference.

In the years following Eli's infant battle with hydrocephalus, she grew into that beautiful, vivacious, and intelligent little girl, bouncing across the rostrum at her daddy's law school graduation. Seven years earlier, my husband and I saw graduation from an elite law school as a momentous prelude to doing good in a troubled world. After all we had been through, the pomp and circumstance mattered so little to us when it finally came. Of course, I still hope my husband will do such good; I still hope *I* will do such good. But as I watched Eli flash happily across the podium, I rejoiced in the lasting good I had already done in *her* troubled world.

# THE BEST I HAVE TO GIVE

*by Becca Lloyd*

"So, what do *you* do?" For most people at the party, that question offered the simplest way to get to know their new acquaintance. But after the birth of my oldest son, this question made me look at my toes. Among the tinkling glasses and prosciutto-wrapped hors d'oeurvres at a glittering party for Yale Medical School affiliates, it was awkward to admit that I was a full-time mother.

My husband was a third-year medical student, and his journey to Yale was not the usual tried and true path to the Ivy League. Many of the parents of Shane's classmates, who were also most likely physicians themselves, had enrolled their children in the correct preschool to feed them into the right elementary school, and go on to a high-class prep school that prepared them for an Ivy League undergraduate education, after which, they would go to medical school at Yale. Shane would become the first physician in his family: both Shane and I are no more than two generations away from farmers on every side.

We were obviously different enough without saying a

word. However, while chatting with a neurosurgeon-to-be (daughter of Dr. Neurosurgeon Dad and Dr. Neurosurgeon Mom), I became more self-conscious of my current trajectory. This young medical student had begun plotting her course many years ago (no children in the plans), and, due to my newborn's ever-changing sleep schedule, I was unable to tell her what the next twenty-four hours would be like. I'll never know what she was thinking, but I felt inspected. She was assessing the problem, like a malfunction of the synapses or a misaligned brain stem. In my mind, I heard her say: "Doesn't this girl know that she can do any career she chooses? Where has she been?"

Well, this is where I had been: Shane and I were married just after I graduated with my undergraduate degree at BYU. Two years later, Shane finished his undergraduate degree, while I completed a master's degree in art history. During the first years of marriage, Shane and I worked tirelessly at our schoolwork; the hours of study were only interrupted for meals and our Friday-evening date. We were equally invested in our education and moved in tandem toward successful careers. Shane excelled in science and economics classes, while refining his research skills in biology labs at the university. His grades reflected his dedicated studying, and professors invited him to present his research on the migratory habits of frogs at an international biology conference on the banks of the Amazon River in Manaus, Brazil.

I found my home in graduate school. My classmates were an assortment of former exam-cramming partners, fellow slide library assistants, and study abroad roommates from my undergraduate years. Instead of the memorizing endless lists for multiple-choice exams and pop quizzes that were the norm in traditional undergraduate courses, the graduate curriculum required us to read during the week, talk during class, and write something good at the end. Read, talk, write. My three favorite pastimes. For my job, I assisted professors in class and had my turn up front at the podium as lecturer. Even the images on the screen seemed to be old friends as I described them: Manet, Rembrandt, Massaccio.

As president of the student art history association, I planned activities, lectures, and field trips. My daily routine involved a morning run, grading exams, reading for class, writing term papers, chatting with other grad students while preparing slides for lecture, eating dinner with my new husband, and finishing the night by reading next to him at the kitchen table. I felt blessed to wake up each morning and work in an atmosphere that seemed so well suited for me. I felt validated for my hard work, receiving grants, awards, and leadership responsibilities from the university, as well as being chosen to present at conferences throughout the United States. Our momentum was positive, and both Shane and I received encouragement from our mentors to continue on in our education. Shane made plans for medical school, and I anticipated putting in applications for PhD programs the next winter.

Shane's acceptance at Yale came as a happy surprise. We packed our few humble belongings in a trailer and took our entourage east: Shane, Shane's mom, sister, grandpa, my mom, and I all took turns at the wheel of the family's enormous Ford truck. We felt our "otherness" the instant we stepped out of the truck in New Haven, Connecticut.

The narrow, winding street we stood on was dim from the soaring Gothic towers of the Yale campus fortress. The history and tradition of this place glared us in the eyes, through the menacing gargoyles carved on the library walls. Even without the buildings, there was no escaping the history stored in the very earth of New Haven. The gravestones, rock fences, and ancient trees all whispered to us of an old time; a time without trains and electricity, when the roads were rutted with wagon wheels and horse tracks. Even the summer humidity held the air in place, full of rust, mold, and earth, which lingered like the smell of mothballs in the attic.

We arrived with an acute awareness of our newness; we were from the West, which looked from here to still be in its infancy. And to top it off, Shane and I were twenty-four years old and married. Our first encounter with Shane's classmates at a get-to-know-you barbecue met many raised eyebrows when we revealed our age and married status. A fellow classmate exclaimed, "You are so old for your age!" I didn't have the heart to tell them that we had already been married two years. This was the first of many, many parties upon our arrival. As the weeks went on, Shane and I both started feeling more comfortable and accepted as the faces grew more familiar. Soon enough, we made true friends, and these parties became my favorite part of those early days in New Haven.

Once Shane started school, however, my brief honeymoon with the East Coast was over. I acknowledged the crossroads before me. Everything in my life up to this point had pushed me toward a life in academia, but there was another force guiding me too. While still living in Utah, the topics of my art history research projects in graduate school turned from war and royalty to mothers, babies, and domesticity. I felt drawn to parenting books and magazines and spent my spare moments taking sewing lessons, in hopes of sewing tiny things for tiny bodies. I had made deliberate steps to pursue a PhD program: I had met with a potential advisor in New York who was enthusiastic about my research, I contacted Yale faculty in hopes of auditing courses, and I stacked art journals high on my nightstand. However, before bed, the journals sat untouched, and my efforts to connect with the people who mattered seemed forced and halfhearted. Why did I have to force myself to stop sewing baby hats to return an email regarding art history? Baby hats!

This time was one when I wrestled with the Lord. I prayed. I meditated. I talked with my husband. My prayers began as pleas for guidance and ended as persuasive statements regarding my future in academia. I lovingly received the "stupor" feeling in response, over and over again. I created time lines of how this could be done: if I squeezed in my coursework before baby #1, took exams with a small infant; wrote dissertation before baby #2, wrote articles and applied for jobs during Shane's residency, and on and on. It all seemed so exhausting. One evening, while unpacking boxes in the bedroom, Shane looked at me with great concern, and said, "Becca, if you really want to do this, maybe we could figure out a way for you to go to school and I could help at home with the kids." My stomach lurched. No! We had prayed about Shane's path to medicine and felt spiritual promptings to come to New Haven. Did I feel the same divine confirmation to go on in school? No. Every time I prayed to know if continuing on in school was the right decision, I heard a clear, succinct answer: "Not yet."

It was clear to me that all these plans I had been making would come at a great cost in later years; by studying history as an academic, I would sacrifice the history of my own family. I could imagine the enormous and impossible juggling acts that would become routine between the demands of my career and Shane's unpredictable life as a doctor. I sensed the financial stress that would come to our family with both of us in school and needing to pay enormous daycare fees. I finally understood that if I chose this life, we wouldn't have the luxury of the daily enjoyment of family life and my influence on my own children would be considerably less than I would like. That evening, among the boxes and unbuilt bookcases, I submitted my own will to the will of the Lord. As I prayed, I felt strongly that He wanted me to put my heart into mothering full time. I felt peace, but I couldn't stop the tears from coming. I felt humbled that night, giving up that PhD dream for motherhood, a life that felt so ordinary and plain.

During the weeks that followed, I felt more and more relief about my decision. I realized that in the daydreams of my childhood, I had always imagined myself at home, surrounded by my own children. I grew more excited to be a mother and create a legacy through our home, through teaching the gospel, through traditions and love. I caught the vision of what great potential for good I had in this capacity. After deciding to point my life toward having children, my husband and I resolved to give ourselves two years to prepare for our family. Shane still had ten years of medical training to go, and we agreed that by having me work full time, we could fatten our meager stores and get some school behind us. In the months that followed, I secured a job at the Beinecke Rare Book and Manuscript Library at Yale. In retrospect, I see this job as a compensatory blessing for heeding the promptings the Lord gave me. My employment at the library expanded my interests and understanding of library research immensely while also being a financial support to our family.

Standing there at the medical school party, however, I felt that I stood looking in on my old life from the sidelines. My job at the library at least gave me a workplace and a way to participate in the adult world. But, after I had birthed a beautiful baby boy and quit my job to stay at home with him, I had no employer, no official job title or impressive university affiliation. How was I to answer, "What do you do" to a room full of "doers," who impressively answer this question, "I attend Yale Medical School." I smiled apologetically and replied, "I stay home and take care of our little baby." Both my new acquaintance and I did not know where to go in our conversation from there, and we both found our way to more comfortable, familiar friends.

All the way home, I replayed that answer in my mind: I stay home and take care of our little baby. Does that mean that my professional skill set is shelved far away and I have submitted myself to a lifetime of peek-a-boo and spit-up? Is being a mother at home purely an exercise in sacrifice? As mothers, are we required to trade the excitement and intellectual growth we found in college or the workplace for the monotonous list of daily tasks demanded by our children? Are we to live with the memories of our past lives as vibrant, successful, intelligent women?

Now that I've been a mother a few more years and have another little one, I wish I could tell my "new mother" self at that party to appreciate the immense lessons that I was learning in those fleeting baby days. Caring for a newborn is a time of sacrifice, and the "doing" is a hazy series of physical actions taken to keep the baby growing; there is not much spare time to pick up Spanish or organic chemistry.

However, I received a spectacular emotional education that can only come from caring for a fresh spirit who knows I can care for him, even at times when I wasn't quite sure I could do it. I found that Heavenly Father has blessed the round-the-clock service that I have given to my baby boys by helping my heart love more deeply than ever before. I love my friends, my siblings, my parents, my husband, but because I feel such unrestrained love for my children, I have something remarkable to live for.

My busy toddler turned me from an individual with complete control over my schedule and tasks completed to a flexible, adaptable multitasker who is always (somewhat) prepared for the next adventure. My curious preschooler rekindled my creativity in crayon sessions, my sense of awe as I watched him see the ocean for the first time, and my appreciation for the small, when he has given me a tiny stone or flower that he picked up somewhere on our walk home. In the times of leaving-the-park-but-I-don't-want-to chaos, Heavenly Father has blessed me with fortified patience. Learning this type of patience is a boon to the society at large—no irritating driver, no sloppy waiter, no insensitive cell phone representative can ruffle the feathers of a seasoned parent. We have all seen much worse from an overtired, hungry child. And in those times when my response does not align with my perfectly consistent parenting ideals, Heavenly Father has given my children the ability to instantly forgive, and I humbly start again.

My children have taught me that there will be times when they won't like things that are good for them—they won't like bedtime, they won't like to leave the children's museum, they won't like to share, they won't like to eat the quiche lorraine that I made for dinner—but because I am the mom, it is my responsibility to help them do the things they should by "persuasion, by long-suffering, by gentleness and meekness, and by love unfeigned" (D&C 121:41). For me, this experience of being the grown-up and wanting the best for someone else has been refining. No longer am I someone's child, choosing to do exactly what I want with the time, money, and resources that I have at my disposal. No matter how many "grown-up" experiences I had before I had children, it took becoming a mother, and all that comes with that title, for me to finally grow up.

Now, I am someone's mother, and I feel that the decisions I make contribute to or detract from our family. The kind of person I choose to be today and tomorrow and the day after will have a direct effect on the kind of people my children become. How can I ask for greater purpose than that? The things that seemed so important earlier in life—new clothes, cool phone, fabulous vacations—are overruled by my desire to give all that I have to my children. And I now recognize that the best of what I have to give is not just stuff; the best I have to give is *me*.

As a mother, I see my greatest weaknesses clearly manifest

themselves so that I can address them and I am able to use my strengths to enhance the lives of those most important to me. I'm far from perfect, but this work I am doing brings out the best in me; I can lovingly soothe my fussy babies, my spare moments are filled planning the next family creation, be it popsicle-stick birdhouses or a Peter Pan puppet show, and I smile when I hear my son politely ask for help from another adult, just the way we practice every night around the dinner table.

Parenting also brings out the worst in me. I acknowledge my short attention span when it comes to playing cars, trains, and blocks. I wish I could maintain perfect patience and humor through a tantrum at the end of the day, instead of becoming snappy and frustrated. I wish I could be endlessly entertaining in those long hours when boredom sets in, rather than sneaking away to check my email. The interaction of adults is so civil and predictable: none of my coworkers have ever hit me in the head or recklessly run in the street, with only me to save them. These crazy situations can only be found in the life of a mother with young children, who are most likely telling her at this moment that her breath smells funny and that she isn't reading the story right. These moments challenge me to dig deep, take a breath, and rise above it all as the one adult in the room. And if I don't get it right this time, I'll surely have another opportunity to try again in a few minutes.

So, what do I do all day? I make room in my body for another person to grow. I help a person acquire language, learn how to walk, and gain social confidence. I love other people, and I am loved with no restraints or conditions. I return to the places that I loved as a child and watch my children love to be there too. I go outside in the summertime and play in the snow in the winter. I have a small hand reaching to hold mine when walking to the park. I rock a freshly bathed baby in clean pajamas to sleep at night. I comfort my children when they need someone to hold them while they cry. I celebrate Christmas listening to "Gloooooooo-ria in excelsis Deo" of a little three-year-old voice, while watching his bright eyes see Christmas lights. I have the honor of *being there* for the first smiles, the first steps, the first "I love you, Mama," and all the other most raw, most beautiful human moments that are absolutely impossible to capture secondhand. What do I do all day? I get to be a mom.

# THE RAT RACE

*by Lori Davis*

I don't really like children. I don't hate them either. They can be cute for a while, especially when they're quiet, happy, and someone else's responsibility. But they spend so little time in that state and so much time being loud, demanding chaos creators. So—unlike some women I know—I don't need to hold every baby I see. As a teenager, I sometimes went to great lengths to *avoid* babysitting. In college, elementary education was one of the few majors I never ever considered.

My opinion may not endear me to many women out there, but I'm in good company on this issue. C. S. Lewis, the great children's author, did not like children either. He admitted this as a personal defect, but he still didn't like them.

Given my attitude, the Church's position on motherhood has not always been my favorite part of the gospel. My own mother spent an enormous amount of time on her kids, and she had only two. I was grateful for her efforts, but I didn't see her path working out for me. Who had time to be a full-time mom when there were hundreds of interesting careers out there for the taking? My career aspirations ranged from ballerina to computer programmer to historian to zoologist to teacher of English as a second language (to adults, not children).

Unfortunately for dilettantes like myself, it's easy to have career aspirations, but fulfilling them is something else again. Ballerina fell by the wayside early. Didn't have the body for that. Computer programmer lasted longer, but an internship killed my interest in it. My coworkers, all good programmers, spent their days programming for work and their nights programming for fun. I wanted a life.

My career as a zoologist died on the second day of class at college. Historian lasted until my undergraduate senior thesis, which was enough to burn me on the idea of getting a master's degree. TESOL (teachers of English to speakers of other languages)? Well, I had already graduated by then, and I needed a job right away.

After a year of doing this and that for terrible pay, I landed a job I liked. It was gratifying to receive a regular paycheck that sufficiently supported my husband and me, to receive praise and promotions from my boss, and to put out a professional product. I also enjoyed how impressed many people were by my title and the name of my company. (Those who understood the true nature of my serf-like position were less impressed. "And you *like* that?" one friend asked, incredulously.) Still, it was a good job in many ways, and it could have led to a successful lifetime career.

But that word *career* is a strange one. It comes from the French word *carriére*, which means road, or racecourse—a wild rush done repeatedly, such as a horse in a joust, or the sun across the sky. In other words, it means a rat race. That definition is not nearly as inspiring as those talks we got from high school guidance counselors—the ones about choosing something that inflames our passions and fulfills us, so we can love going to work each morning. I know a woman who tried to comfort a friend after a breakup by saying, "Relationships come and go, but your work will always be there for you." No rat race is as meaningful as this woman implied. There are days in any job when her counsel is about the worst "comfort" I can imagine.

Most people I know don't have careers, at least not in that inspiring, take-on-the-world kind of way. Most people just have jobs. They show up every morning because they need the money. The lucky ones enjoy some of what they do, but they certainly wouldn't show up every morning, day in, day out, for free. Almost any job becomes a rat race by degenerating into more or less the same thing over and over again. All jobs have their tedious tasks, their annoying coworkers, and their disappointing lack of pay raises. Even those lucky few who succeed in a career that sounds fulfilling—something like music, sports, or drama, for instance—often find that those careers also become just a job.

When it comes to jobs, men are generally believed to earn more and move up the ranks faster than women. But there is one way in which I think women are luckier than men. Our society enables and encourages us to pursue careers, but many of us can also quit and stay home with our children. Very few men get that choice. It's a hard decision to make, and sometimes having no option might seem easier. But in general, I think it's better to have a choice: I was able to enjoy my serf status in the company because I knew I didn't have to stay there until I turned sixty-five.

Four years into my so-called career, I quit to become a stay-at-home mom. My husband had supported me in my job, and he supported me in quitting as well. Then I found out that my high school guidance counselor wasn't the only one I had misunderstood. People in the Church always talk about motherhood in glorified terms: it's the women's counterpart to the priesthood, an enormously fulfilling responsibility, a great spiritual trust, and so forth. No one ever mentioned that there is no rat race as round-the-clock repetitious as keeping an infant fed, rested, and clean.

I didn't find early motherhood to boost my spirituality in the slightest. I didn't have time for spiritual things. Gone were the monthly temple trips, the half hour of morning scripture study, the energy for compassionate service and my calling. For the first little while, I didn't even get to partake of the sacrament. My prayers were fervent only because I was endlessly repeating, "Please, Lord, just make her sleep!"

The sleep situation gradually improved, and some of those spiritual things crept back into my life, but I still lacked the very things that had made my previous job fulfilling. I received no paycheck, no promotions, and no professional results. Moreover, absolutely no one was impressed by my title. Motherhood may be a rat race at times, but it isn't a career; it's just life—life at its rawest and most basic. Vital functions like eating, sleeping, cleaning, and entertaining escalate into an overwhelming amount of work, in complete disregard of normal business hours and the legal minimum wage.

But as I've wiped up messes and dried silly tears, I've realized that children aren't the only ones who spend a large part of their time being loud, demanding, chaos creators. I sometimes wonder if Heavenly Father grows weary of holding my hand through every little step. Maybe He tires of cleaning up my disasters, listening to my temper-tantrum prayers, and telling me things He's told me a thousand times before. If we are here on earth to become more like Him, nothing trains us better than motherhood, for we are working long, hard hours doing precisely what He does, not just day in, day out, but eternity in, eternity out.

So far as I've heard, Heavenly Father doesn't receive a paycheck either. His rewards are more subtle and less certain, and of those, I've had an abundance too: the first time my baby smiled, the first time she laughed, the first time she spoke, the first time she shared, the first time she sang. These rewards are mostly invisible to the outside observer, but they are more fulfilling than anything I received during my career. A paycheck, after all, is soon spent and no matter how much it is, it's rarely enough. But my daughter is here in my family to stay, even beyond death, and she never stops learning and growing and changing. Nor does she ever stop demanding that I learn and grow and change. She has pointed out so many ways in which I am not yet much like my Heavenly Father: my patience is not infinite, my creativity has limits, and my selflessness has a long way to go. She challenges me to develop these qualities in a way that no job has ever demanded.

I think it is no mistake that Church leaders talk about the glory of motherhood, rather than the drudgery. Who would choose to lose health, sleep, money, and leisure time, not to mention sanity, if that was what they emphasized in general conference? And yet even I, the mother who doesn't like children, would never trade my child in to have those things back. The Church prods us to become more like Christ through many painful experiences (callings and missions and motherhood among them), and they do it by holding out the glorious end result for us to admire. The end result of my motherhood is not one but two infinitely precious daughters of God, as my daughter and I both pursue our own exaltation.

As my own daughter has grown, I've discovered a secret—something that might surprise C. S. Lewis if he were still alive: Parenthood is nothing like babysitting. My own child is nothing like other people's children. A babysitter never sees that glorious end result and those moments of reward along the way. A mother works infinitely harder but understands the value of what she's working for. I am certain that I got the cutest, brightest, most wonderful child who ever lived. Even in those moments where she may appear to be nothing but a loud, demanding, chaos creator, *I* know it isn't true. She is mine, and that makes a world of difference.

# AGAINST ALL ODDS

*by Marianne Kraczek*

Motherhood was not on my mind the summer I took a temporary receptionist position at a large international communications company in suburban Washington, DC. I was nineteen and had finished my first year of college. When I found out I would be answering phones for the vice president of public relations, I was thrilled. I was a journalism major at that time and was considering an emphasis in public relations. The VP exemplified a high-powered career woman and had the wardrobe to match: dry-clean only suits and name-brand shoes. When she was in her large corner office with a wall of windows, she was always busy meeting with important people. She was also often away on business.

Sitting outside her office at the receptionist's desk, I pictured myself with her job. I wondered if I would enjoy it and if this was the path to pursue. I found time to talk to her about working in public relations, and we discussed internship opportunities. I also worked. Since this was before cell phones and Blackberries were in everyone's hands, I took all of her calls and learned when to interrupt her, when to take a message, and when to pretend I was taking a message.

It was when her little boy called that I started to think not about career tracks but about motherhood. He was about six years old. He called all of the time for his mother, but I always answered the phone. Often I was able to immediately transfer the call, but just as often I had to tell this boy that his mother was busy, either in a meeting or out to lunch or on the phone with someone else. When I would tell the VP that her son was on the phone again, I could see some anguish and wondered what she was thinking.

Then I thought of my own mother who stayed at home with me. I took for granted that she was always there. She was there when I came home from school. She was available to take me to lessons or to a friend's house. She spent time with me when I needed her. When I called her, she always answered the phone.

After six weeks working as the receptionist and a child's go-between, I decided that whatever it took, I was going to stay home with my children. I had a lot of time to think about that decision. It was ten years before motherhood became a reality for me, and I had no idea how difficult it would be to stick to the decision I made at nineteen.

I went back to college that fall and later felt impressed to change my major. Instead of working in public relations, after graduating from college I taught social studies and publications at a high school in Las Vegas. My future husband, Mike, was the theater teacher. We were friends for some time before we started dating. When he told me about his plans to attend graduate school, I knew I was in love when I felt sad at the thought of him leaving me behind. Fortunately, he didn't want to leave me behind either.

Shortly after our marriage, Mike started applying to graduate programs around the country. While I supported his decision to go, I was concerned about starting a family. Already in my late twenties, I had a strong desire to be a mother. I was impatient and didn't want to wait another three years. I instinctively felt Heavenly Father would not have us wait long either.

Remembering the promise I made to myself to stay home with my children, we discussed options for mixing parenthood and graduate studies. There were no easy solutions. With these thoughts weighing on us, we decided to delay baby plans until we knew where we were going. To prepare ourselves for the changes ahead, we started living on one income and saving as much money as possible.

When Mike was accepted to the Yale School of Drama, he almost turned the offer down. The cost of tuition worried him. Yale offered only limited financial support. Other schools offered tuition and stipend grants, and we could have avoided more debt. My husband, always conservative with money, nearly walked away from an amazing educational opportunity.

The biggest concern he had about attending Yale was how to afford a family while attending the most demanding technical design program in the country. Logically, the idea made no sense, but we both felt the impression that New Haven was where we belonged. We moved forward unsure of how we were going to do it all but believing that it would work out somehow.

The Yale School of Drama (YSD) was an amazing place to learn theater, but it wasn't family friendly. Unlike most of the other professional schools at Yale, YSD offered no financial aid budget for married students or their families. Students were not permitted to hold an outside job during the school year because of the intensity of the program. Loans and scholarships allotted us enough money for one person to live on—and live tightly. The reality was that only a small number of married students attended the school. Everybody knew that marriages often didn't last at YSD. Separations were common and often led to divorce. This pattern mirrored that of the professional theater world where the motto is, "The show must go on," even at the expense of personal lives. Theater professionals and students work days, nights, and weekends. Time that is usually dedicated to family is spent on a production instead.

While married students were rare, babies were unheard of. What crazy people would try to have a baby while in graduate school at YSD? Well, we did. I worked our first year in New Haven and got pregnant during that time. While I was on campus one day, a long-time professor looked at my swollen belly and said, "I don't think we have had a baby at the drama school in thirty years!"

I was excited for impending motherhood, but Mike was stressed. He didn't have the same excitement when the baby kicked or when we went to our ultrasound. His prayers were filled with pleas for help to support a wife and child and keep up with school. We had significant savings to help subsidize our budget, but survival still looked impossible. Because no one in Mike's program could show us how to do it, I looked for hope in the many other parents in our ward who were also in a similar situation. I thought somehow if they could do it, so could we. I tried to have faith that our Heavenly Father would help us because we were doing the right thing.

My husband endured a grueling schedule. Classes started at 9:00 a.m. and went until 2:00 p.m. At 2:00, production assignments started. There were always a few plays in the works at any given time. Work and rehearsals would continue until about 10:00 p.m. After rehearsals, the actors went home, but the technical designers had to stay to make tech notes and fix problems. This lasted until about midnight or later, and then Mike could come home. Oh, and there was homework too. With all of this responsibility, Mike's biggest challenge was making time for family and church. During production assignments, we went great lengths of time without seeing each other except for Sundays. Mike committed to not working on Sunday unless he absolutely had to. I believe that the Lord blessed him for this and expanded his capabilities.

When I was four months pregnant, I lost my job. I agonized over how I was going to find another. At the same time, Mike calculated our taxes and realized that we owed a lot of money in tithing. While he didn't think twice about paying it, I couldn't stop thinking about how much we needed that money. Among other expenses, I needed maternity clothes and had no money to buy any. We paid the tithing, but I admit that I did it grudgingly. A few days later, I was called back to work and rehired. They had found more work for me. They also promised to keep me employed until I had my baby. I learned—again—that God will support us in keeping His commandments.

Small blessings added up like raindrops in a bucket. I discovered that my sister had kept all of her baby equipment, toys, and clothes even though she was done having children. For years, she had been holding on to those things for me. I was elated and so thankful. When Mike and I did have to buy things, we were blessed to find them at a price we could afford. We found a slightly used high chair at a tag sale. It had been left out in the rain the night before, and because it looked dirty, the owner sold it to us for just four dollars. When we cleaned it up, it looked brand new. We didn't have new things; in fact, the only new things we had were gifts, but everything was in good condition. We felt blessed to have spent so little and still have all we needed and more.

When fall semester started our second year, the dean hosted a school-wide party. I was nine months pregnant and waddling. The dean lived at the top of a large hill, and I could barely make the walk up the driveway. When we finally arrived at the party, I felt like a circus sideshow act. I could have not been more out of place. I did my best to be friendly while brushing off the stares, the eye-rolls, and the hushed comments. Some people were supportive and excited for us, especially the ones from Mike's class. But it was apparent at that party that many others were judging us.

Motherhood finally came. The anticipation didn't prepare me for the divine joy our daughter would bring. She was worth everything. All the sacrifices we made seemed small in comparison to the happiness I felt taking care of and loving her. Sometimes I put off everything else just to hold her a little longer. Her smiles made me forgive sleepless nights and endless diapers. Having her fulfilled me in a way nothing else could. Even my husband, who questioned beginning a family at this time, was overwhelmed with joy.

I was committed to staying home with our daughter, but I still had fears of what life as a stay-at-home mom would be like. Would I be lonely? Would I miss working? The reality was that I was happier than I had ever been. Good friends helped. I lived in a community of graduate student families, both members and nonmembers. The moms I met befriended me and taught me techniques and skills that helped me learn how to care for a baby. We relied on each other when our husbands were busy with classes and assignments and we had no other family nearby. Common experiences bonded us. We babysat for each other and held playdates, more for us than for our children. We had great conversations and discussed current events, religion, and books. We lived in apartments that were falling apart, and most of us had very few nice things, but we had great times, and I learned that that is how being a stay-at-home mom should be. We should support each other as much as possible.

I am still amazed at how we lived off of so little. When money became especially tight and we didn't know how to pay rent, a blessing would come in the form of a tax credit, a gift from a parent, or an unexpected grant. We always got by and still had enough for some luxuries, like traveling and an occasional Broadway show.

The divine help we received became clear by the end of the school year. Many of the single YSD students started to take out additional loans to survive until the end of the semester. We didn't need (or want) any more financial aid. Our ability to stretch out our finances surprised other students, and they started asking how we did it. We had no logical answers: we just knew our prayers had been answered.

In our second and third year at Yale, more married students entered the technical design program. When they saw we had a baby, they started asking questions. By then I had information to share. I knew about resources on and off campus for families, and I shared my personal tips for living lean. Another YSD spouse and I started a group for spouses and significant others connected specifically to YSD. We created a handbook with information about Yale, the drama school, and living in New Haven. With permission from the assistant dean at YSD, we became an official group and met regularly for support, fun, and information.

Mike and I decided to expand our family again, and I became pregnant with our second baby during Mike's third and final year. This time I was not the only pregnant wife; at least two other YSD couples were expecting, and another married couple had just welcomed their first baby. After we left, every married couple we knew at YSD had children while in school. We started at Yale uncertain if we could start a family and get through graduate school, but we trusted God to help us. We had no idea that we could do that and start a baby boom too. Incredibly, the drama school is now friendlier to families, and pregnant wives and children are not such an oddity.

Many times we never know why we are prompted to do things, especially when it doesn't make sense at the time. But recently I went to a doctor's appointment and learned that because of a condition I have, my fertility is declining much more rapidly than normal. While thinking about this news,

I thought of our experiences, seven years ago, as new parents in graduate school. What if we had waited? Would I have all three of my children? I am grateful when I think about the promptings and desire to start having children at that time. It is comforting to know we have a source of inspiration that sees our future more clearly and guides us.

I have no regrets about my decision to be a stay-at-home mom. Although our finances are not as stretched as they used to be, we still make material sacrifices in order to live on one income. We don't live in the biggest house, we don't drive new cars, and we are careful about what we spend money on. There are moments when I miss working, and sometimes I envy a friend who has accomplished great things in the professional world. When I feel this way, I remember that life can be lived in seasons. I will never get back this time I have with my young children, and I enjoy the freedom to serve them without restrictions that come from outside work. I can hold my child's hand at the school bus stop and be there when she gets home. I can drop other plans when they get sick. I have time to make healthy meals. I can enjoy childhood again from their perspective, and I have no guilt about not spending quality time with them. I'm not the mother trapped in an office who needs an assistant to tell her child that she can't talk to him. I know they will grow up fast, and when they do, it will be my turn to attend graduate school.

# THE MOST WONDERFUL THING IN THE WORLD

*by Addie LaDuke*

I thought my biggest challenge that summer would be soldiering through the heat as a pregnant woman in Arizona. But something was off. The doctor was concerned because I was measuring bigger than I should have, and I was very sick, more so than I had ever been in previous pregnancies. I could hardly get off the sofa to feed my family. At one point while driving to a doctor's appointment, my nausea overcame me on the freeway; I was forced to turn home to clean up the mess and skip the appointment. My husband helped me all he could, but he was working ten- to twelve-hour days, six days a week, as a summer clerk at his law firm. We were living with our two daughters in a small, furnished condo in Phoenix, away from our home in Tucson and away from the support of our ward.

We found out that summer that the baby I was carrying was sick too. He had a genetic irregularity that made his little body incompatible with life. So along with my sickness, I felt heartache and anxiety. My husband and I do not get pregnant as easily as some, and we wanted a miracle more than anything. The summer ended with a miracle, but not the one that we expected: I survived. Our baby's heart stopped just before it was necessary for the doctors to take him out of the womb to save me. After a week's stay in the hospital, I was sent home with more bad news. Due to the complications I experienced, my doctor would have to continue to monitor a hormone in my blood. Unless I wanted to risk more serious complications, I would not be able to get pregnant again until the hormone completely disappeared from my blood and remained gone for six months to a year.

Life at that time didn't afford me much time to recover from these blows. The day after my discharge from the hospital in Phoenix, we had to pack for our home in Tucson, about a two-hour drive. On our way home, we stopped at the lab to have the first of many tests done. I brought my eighteen-month-old daughter in with me. She was sure to cause trouble waiting in the car with her dad and sister, plus I needed a little time to try to cuddle with her after my week away in the hospital. Normally an adorable, friendly child with bright blue eyes and curly blonde hair, she was not looking her best. She had ketchup on her shirt and a chocolate milk stain all over the back of her pants from our lunch stop. She was also starting to emit high-pitched screeches, a sure sign that nap time had arrived.

Another little girl about her age sat in the waiting room. Enthroned in her mother's lap she pointed to things in the room and called out words to name them. "Chair! Water! Girl!" She commanded the stage, and the four or five others in the room admired her little performance. In an attempt to steal the show, my daughter walked over to the trash can and reached in, all the while looking in my direction to get me to stop her. I walked over to grab her and make her sit quietly in my lap, but she screamed, "NO MAMA, WALK, WALK"—over and over. Her cries echoed out into the hall and down the stairs. I remember wishing my husband would hear them from the car and come save me. Just then, a technician called my name from the back of the lab. "Ms. LaDuke?"

We stood up. I decided to strap my daughter in her stroller so she could not wreak havoc on her surroundings. "NOOOO!" she screeched in a voice loud enough to break glass. Maybe this time my husband would hear her. *How could so much voice come from such a little body?* As we walked into the lab, a waft from her body told me she needed a diaper change. (In retrospect, this may have been why she did not want to sit down.) There was not much I could do but wait to solve her uncomfortable problem when my test was done.

The lab technician who called my name was a lanky cowboy type in his mid-twenties, more suited for Wranglers than scrubs. I apologized for my daughter, who at this time was screaming "Holdy, Holdy," while reaching in my direction. The stench from her diaper was now apparent to anyone within a five-foot radius.

"Is this your only one?" the technician asked, observing our troubled state. I explained I had another one who was four, also a girl. "My girlfriend really wants kids someday," he said, "but I am not sure." He pointed to a picture pinned to the wall of him in a cowboy hat with a very pretty blonde. Then he paused for a minute. "Tell me the truth, is it worth it to have kids?"

I wondered how I looked to him. Not only was I struggling to control my daughter, but I was weak and pale from losing a lot of blood during the surgery. My black hair only emphasized the translucence of my skin. My iron and potassium counts were low from the loss of blood, so I had difficulty lifting things because of my lack of energy and muscle cramps. I had also just used almost all my energy to help clean our apartment and pack our belongings in the car. I must have looked tired and pathetic. The lab technician could not have known any of what I had been through. I had sacrificed just about everything in an effort to expand my family. Yet I think he was thinking to himself, "Wow, parenthood takes a toll on people."

My answer to his question was short and simple. I looked at him and said, "I am not going to lie to you and say that it is easy." That was stating the obvious considering my screaming child and corpse-like appearance—something he had probably observed in other tired parents. I looked at my wailing toddler, then turned to the technician and said—with the most sincere and determined look I could give, "But it *is* the *most* wonderful thing in the world."

That was it. The lab test was over, and the conversation ended with cordial good-byes. I rushed out to find a place to change my daughter's diaper.

Though we did not look pretty that day, and we were not making it look fun, my eternal family is the greatest blessing I have on this earth. How could I have expressed to this young man the love that I felt for my child from the first moment I held her? It was a love that was overwhelming but one that only faintly echoed the way our Heavenly Father feels for us. Motherhood, for me, has been otherworldly. Almost daily I am taught to love more purely and to realize how much love our Heavenly Father has for us. This kind of growth always makes me feel closer to my heavenly home.

I am sure that this young man feels love for his girlfriend. Yet I wanted to say to him that I don't think the love between a man and a woman can teach us all aspects of God's love. We are His children, and as parents, we can learn the depth of His sacrifices for our success. It seems logical to me that for us to truly understand that love and sacrifice, we need to experience love for something as helpless, innocent, and free-willed as a child. Even though I relish the hugs and kisses and the moments of accomplishment, I will never forget how hard those first few weeks of parenthood were. All of a sudden I had to grow from a selfish being, who only had to make little compromises to maintain a happy marriage, to a mother, who had to work nonstop to maintain the life of someone else. For me, this transition has been essential to my understanding of God's pure love for us. Through it, I gained so many opportunities to practice Christlike love and sacrifice here on earth, and I've caught a glimpse into our glorious and productive future. Parenthood constitutes a great part of my eternal progression and typifies what our heavenly family will be like when we return home. My experiences just prior to this conversation in the lab had been a considerable lesson on sacrifice and love. Understanding the love of God is not something I would like to miss, nor do I think it should be something that the technician—or anyone—shrugs off because it seems hard. Part of the greatness of parenthood is the growth it affords the members of the family.

I did not know how to express to this young man that the role of motherhood has helped me to grow and mature in ways I never thought possible. I am forced into situations that test me to be a little kinder, more patient, and—maybe even the technician could attest—more long-suffering. As a parent, I have learned fast that our children show us our faults by mirroring them. I can remember realizing, as I watched my then-three-year-old yell, "Hurry up, Mom!" while stomping her foot, that this child was learning impatience from me. How quickly I seek to repent when I see the bad seeds I am planting. Yet when I plant the right seeds, both my children and I are blessed.

If this young technician chooses not to have children, he will miss out on so many blessings. Some of my greatest blessings have come while teaching my children the gospel. Helping them feel the Spirit strengthens me and my testimony, creating a circle of blessings. Both child and parent are blessed by good efforts. One morning while I was loading my children in the car, my oldest daughter said to me, "Mom, I want to feel the Spirit this morning. Can we please listen to church music?" What joy I felt in knowing that our daughter was seeking a connection to our Heavenly home. No wonder God commanded Adam and Eve to multiply and replenish the earth, for in so doing our love multiplies and our hearts are replenished. Creating an eternal family is the closest we come to our heavenly home while in this world. This feeling comes in the tiniest of moments, like when our youngest eagerly points to pictures of the Savior and says, "Jesus Chwist" or when she runs to give me a hug after I return from the store and squeals, "Mama, I wub you." How could my heart be any more full?

The world offers many things to fill a person's life, but few that really fill her heart. This cowboy has probably pondered how fun, free, inexpensive, and easy a life without the responsibility of children could be. He wouldn't have to deal with dirty diapers or screaming children. I wonder if he ponders what the end of such a life might leave him. I know I could have focused on a lot of other paths in my life—wealth, fame, beauty, security, ease, or a combination of them all. While some of these may still be secondary goals, where would any of these get me in the eternal scheme of things? None of these goals could bring me true happiness, nor could any of them last beyond the grave. If I had made these other paths primary goals and skipped parenthood altogether, I know eventually I would look back on my life and see that I had traded eternal blessings for a life of worldly distractions—a mess of pottage for a birthright (Genesis 25:29–34). While there are plenty of trials in family life, I know that they only make us stronger as we work through them. Even in my weakest moments, when life is not looking pretty, I know my family here on earth brings me closer to my Heavenly Father day by day. I know that this is the path that brings me the most joy.

"Is it worth it to have kids?" I think the lab technician may have been surprised by my answer: "It *is* the most wonderful thing in the world."

# MODELED AND MOLDED

*by Lia Collings*

Baby showers have never been my thing. I can do without the pacifier-shaped cookies, the games ("Guess what's in *this* label-less jar of baby food!"), or the one-upmanship from sisters who brandish handmade gifts and scrapbooked cards in designer gift bags. In fact, I came hog-tied or blind-sided to all three of the showers for my daughters. But the shower for Leigh's baby was different; I couldn't wait to go to that one.

It wasn't that I loved Leigh more than my other friends or her baby more than my own children. Nor had I stumbled upon a pattern for an attractive set of baby leg warmers that would wow all the other moms, earning me a place with the crafty elite of the ward. Mostly, I looked forward to this shower because Leigh's older sister, Claire, was hosting it—in her own home—and I had admired this woman from afar for quite a while.

I first met Claire at a party that Leigh and her husband had hosted to celebrate their newly remodeled home. Claire and I were both pregnant mommies trying to keep our young children on this side of disaster as they careened wildly through the immaculate apartment. The similarities between us ended there. For one thing, Claire handled her three boys far better than I handled my two girls. Her gentle but firm commands seemed always to summon obedience where my incessant pleadings rarely did.

Though Claire's conversation subdued children, it enlivened adults. She quickly proved herself one of those people for whom "small talk" is impossible because nothing about her talk was small; her ideas, experiences, understanding—even vocabulary—were so lofty, it was impossible not to be elevated by them.

Her heights didn't confine themselves to conversation. She was a striking 5'10" beauty. I later told my husband that even in her pregnant state, Claire would be my model if I ever had to paint a Greek goddess. (I never did.) She had a PhD in Russian literature and now channeled her talents and energies into family, mothering three active sons full time while her husband completed his residency. She explained this as though there could be nothing more natural in the world, a lack of tension I found as unusual as it was admirable. Claire impressed me in every point.

I had infrequent and random encounters with my new idol after that party, but each one substantiated my initial impressions of her. She passed along news of children's theater productions, started up a music and movement playgroup, and sent two of her young sons with their father to a bass trombone concert. At the recital, her six-year-old waved and pointed from the balcony when a bassoon marched on stage to accompany the trombone—evidence that Claire must have discussed this and other instruments with him at home. In every point she seemed a cut above—or at least a breaking-apart-from—the norm. Yes, a chance to see this goddess in her dedicated temple made me look forward to this baby shower like none other.

Initially, she did not disappoint. Our hostess received us graciously, and we entered her home to the smell of a butternut squash soup simmering on the stove. A flawlessly executed chocolate truffle cake stood prominently on the table, and a nineteenth-century-looking blessing gown stretched artfully across a wooden cradle. I learned later that Leigh, the honoree of the evening, had made it herself.

I discreetly placed my present, wrapped in last Sunday's comic section, into the cradle, crossing my fingers that the newspaper print wouldn't bleed into the sheets. (The designer gift bags harboring the other presents made fine bedfellows for it.) Glancing over my shoulder to be sure no one had noticed the casting of my mite, I shuffled away to find a seat. As I nestled into the sofa, admiring a pair of heirloom booties sitting on the mantle across from me, I let my eyes wander upward to the print on the wall just above them.

And then I jumped. Startled, disconcerted, maybe even a bit embarrassed, I instinctively turned away from the image. I felt my cheeks start to burn.

In this home to four developing boys our hostess had placed over the mantel *not* the picture of Christ often seen in Mormon homes, nor the more obscure but personally loved painting of Christ I might have expected from her. Instead she had placed a semi-nude, frontal portrait of a beautiful young mother nursing her infant. My faith in Claire's superior ways was too strong to be easily shaken; I trusted that she would not hang such a portrait unwittingly. What did she intend?

I wondered all night. As the evening progressed, I glanced at the print occasionally—Picasso's *Maternity, 1905*, I later learned. But a round of "talking shop" kept my mind occupied. To play the game we took turns answering the thoughtful questions about motherhood that our winning hostess had provided. The crowd gave me a lot to think about.

I listened to a Metropolitan Opera singer tell how the birth of her son had changed her life to center on the small accomplishments of another. As she spoke I imagined how others in her field must have balked at her decision to have a child at all. Certainly few others had chosen to become mothers, especially at her young stage of career building.

I knew that the single, Jamaican-born mother struggled every day to help her two beautiful teenage daughters and handsome teenaged son rise above their inner-city New Haven surroundings. In other settings she had confided her occasional guilt that she hadn't let her children do all the extracurricular activities their friends did. And yet, her close-knit family and her children's strong testimonies, she said, assured her that if she had erred, she had done so on the side of right.

The mothers in the room didn't redefine only the world's definition of womanhood and motherhood. Each of them fashioned the mold of "good mothering" to her own liking, independent even of Mormon cultural norms. One mother who had worked for LDS Social Services taught sacrifice and compassion to her five-year-old by encouraging him to donate the gifts he received at his birthday party to a local shelter for women and children. Another mother studying art history used books of great religious paintings to help her eighteen-month-old think about Jesus during the sacrament.

Listening to these women, I came to see Claire's self-assurance in hanging her Picasso as a manifestation of the self-assurance I observed from all of them. These mothers possessed a quiet confidence that reminded me of the faith described by Joseph Smith. Faith, he said, is "an actual knowledge" to any person, "that the course of life which [she] is pursuing is according to His will."[13] Each of these women seemed to possess such faith, not only in her life course, but also in her ability to be a good mother. Though their paths varied widely, each of these women exuded a quiet confidence that her current life course conformed to the Lord's plan for her. Furthermore, aside from following basic guidelines from Church leaders on their home duties, they didn't look to some cultural or societal norm to show them how to rear their children. They looked to the Lord and their own unique experiences. And they shared an underlying faith that the Lord would use those experiences and talents to make them successful in their families.

My final viewing of that nursing mother left me with mixed impressions. In some ways, the picture, which at first challenged my esteem for Claire and her mothering, left me even firmer in my admiration. I believed that Claire, in her characteristic wisdom, had a vision in placing that image so prominently before her sons. Knowing that they would come of age in a world that "objectifies [women] and disrespects them and then suggests that they are able to leave their mark on mankind only by seduction," she put before them from their earliest hours an image of woman in her highest and holiest calling—that of mother—and then personified that holiness everyday in her own life.[14]

But in other ways the prominent Picasso print knocked my polar star out of position. In every previous encounter with Claire, I had left wishing I could be more like her. Though I had no desire to fit the "good mom" mold of creating a new hairdo for my daughters everyday or providing them with a riveting pipe-cleaner craft after school each week, I would have loved to be the good mom who frequented children's theater and schooled my children in lesser-known orchestra instruments. But I would never hang that Picasso print, even in my home of all girls.

Sitting at the proverbial feet of this breast-feeding woman, I pondered the lives of the women sitting with me and considered the ways that their quiet confidence made them—and their mothering—different from me. I would never be a star contralto like my opera friend, and my children would get most of their Puccini from YouTube, not a New York stage. I didn't know where to *get* a medieval painting quiet book, much less what to tell my children about it. I just couldn't be that kind of amazing mother.

But I could be my own kind of amazing mother. In reflecting on the differences, I'd almost missed the similarity that all but eclipsed those differences: each of us was trying her hardest to be the mother that God wanted her to be. Each of us looked to the same Guide and Source in our efforts to strengthen our families.

I had gone to this shower in hopes of observing a good

model up close and copying her. I left the party with a model firmly in place, but not the one I had expected. Listening to those mothers that night—all of whom I admired and wished to be like in various ways—I realized that I could certainly change elements of my mothering as I was inspired by the models I saw around me. But, ultimately, God didn't want me to copy any model but the perfect one—the Savior. My faith, my quiet confidence, lay in His ability to take whatever raw material I laid before Him and mold it into the mother He and my children needed me to be.

# LET THE CHILDREN COME

*by Georgia Bonney*

A friend recently asked me, "What makes you tick? Why do you do what you do?" As a mother of fourteen children, I thought these were excellent questions. When I think of the next meal always pressing, the laundry mounting, the dishes waiting, and—inevitably—the disagreements multiplying, I sometimes ask myself the same question. Why do I do this? Why did I sign up for this?

Here I am, a recipient of two graduate degrees from the University of Southern California, a National Merit and a Fulbright Scholar, and an author of several publications, raising this large family in a world that discounts families. I am a mother in a world that mocks the woman who decides to forego a career and take on mothering as a full-time calling. It is clear to me that Satan has skewed the priorities of our society. He has used the media to degrade essential stages of life: courtship, marriage, childbearing, and childrearing. For a woman to work day after day, year after year, at building a righteous family in this environment, she must have great courage. Raising a family with strong roots in the gospel, a thirst for knowledge, and a passion for the good and the beautiful is a herculean effort.

I have not always concentrated on family. Starting piano studies at age three, I studied music passionately, performing, competing, and winning national and international competitions throughout my youth. I pursued my musical studies in college and graduate school, a path that culminated in a core Fulbright scholarship to Vienna. It was during graduate school that I met Philip. Since I was not a member of the Church at that time, Philip introduced me to the missionaries, the Book of Mormon, and copies of many general conference talks. After some lively missionary discussions and much prayer, I knew I needed to be baptized. Philip and I were married shortly afterward and spent our first year of marriage in Vienna while I completed my Fulbright studies. When we returned to the United States, we were expecting our first child. I continued to publish and teach university classes, but I sensed a difficult decision looming in my future. Would this child become the center of my life, or would my career take precedence?

As I prayed over my decision to accept full-time motherhood over a career, Jesus's words, "Let the children come," (Mark 10:14) struck me as no others ever had. These were the same words I read in a talk by Spencer W. Kimball: "They should live together normally and let the children come."[15] I knew I could continue my career with only one child, considering all the childcare options available. But this was not how the Lord intended my family to exist. I thought about the counsel he gave to Adam and Eve: "Be fruitful, and multiply, and replenish the earth" (Genesis 1:28). The evidence was clear and unrelenting. I would set aside my career, and we would let the children come.

The children came quickly! Six children arrived in fast succession. By the eighth pregnancy, prenatal visits had become so tedious and time-consuming to me that it wasn't until the day we were packing up our home to move that I submitted to an ultrasound. I was almost eight months pregnant at the time. Imagine my husband's surprise, as he stood surrounded by little children, packers, and piles of boxes, when I arrived home and announced, "Honey! It's not one baby, it's TWINS!" The children were delighted and felt extremely blessed. And the Lord continued to bless us . . . more abundantly than we imagined. A year later, we went in for another ultrasound (which my husband made sure to attend), only to find that we were expecting twins again, this time fraternal. The day I returned home from the hospital with Rebekah and Joseph, we had eleven children, five under the age of three. Excitement soon gave way to exhaustion.

The following years were joyous, but a lot of work. Philip's new job as a basic training commander consumed him for sixty to eighty hours a week, and I struggled to maintain an orderly home with so many little children. During this same time, my oldest daughter was diagnosed with juvenile dermatomyositis, or inflammation of the blood vessels, a horrible disease with a 40 percent mortality rate. Physically incapacitated in various ways, my daughter demanded much attention. Weekly doses of chemotherapy and heavy prednisone weakened her condition as it waged war on the illness. I endured two painful miscarriages. The days seemed endless. My testimony of motherhood began to falter. I began to wonder why I had worked so hard to accomplish so much in music, performing, publishing, and teaching, so I could change diapers, run laundry, and rarely leave the house. I became confused. Academia beckoned me. It wasn't feasible for me to do anything immediately, but I thought perhaps I could look into long-distance learning and pursue a PhD.

It took many weeks for me to realize that I was not truly seeking a return to academia; rather, I was seeking emancipation from my role as mother. Neal A. Maxwell described me when he said, "Some mothers in today's world feel 'cumbered' by home duties and are thus attracted by other more 'romantic' challenges. Such women could make the same error of perspective and priorities that Martha made. The woman, for instance, who deserts the cradle in order to help defend civilization against the barbarians may well later meet, among the barbarians, her own neglected child."[16] I did not want my children to suffer the consequences of my selfish choices. Once I accepted, yet again, that I needed to follow the Lord's path for me, which quite obviously was to raise these children, the mists of darkness lifted, and my life became more joyful. All my studies had not been in vain; they just needed to be channeled into my work with the children. Rather than mope and grumble over the tedious chores, I tried altering my mind-set to be productive, creative, and enlightened.

As I recommitted to follow the divine mandate to raise my children in righteousness, I found that Heavenly Father not only helped me through the rigors of motherhood at that difficult time, but he used every bit of the talents and abilities that I brought to the table as a mother. With prayer,

I created a better schedule and budget. My focus shifted to education: researching new companies with educational toys (and learning to bargain shop for them online), exploring home school curricula to supplement my children's public school education, and reading book anthologies to find the best literature to share as a family. I studied the Cub Scout, Boy Scout, and Young Women programs, which my children were involved in, and helped my children set goals. I served as Primary president, where I better learned the importance of grounding children in the gospel. Heavenly Father had channeled my passion for music and academia into my child-raising skills without my even realizing it.

Spiritually, my mind was opened to revelation. At a time when I felt that my childbearing years might be ending, our bishop one day proudly displayed a new painting of Esther for our ward building, I had the distinct feeling that we would be blessed with one more baby girl. One year later, our beautiful Esther joined the family.

Around the time of Esther's birth, Philip and I were preparing for a post in Senegal (our tenth move, second overseas), a change that would relocate our family to the westernmost tip of Africa. To prepare for that move, we attended the Oakland Temple. As Philip and I attended the endowment session, I had the most distinct feeling that there would be another little boy, and that his name was to be Peter. Doubting the prompting, I asked the Lord if this could be true, only to have the impression strike me twice more. What a feeling of elation accompanied this divine communication! But this child was not to be born of my womb. Upon our arrival in Dakar, Senegal, before we were even unpacked, my husband received orders to leave for his first business trip. Imagine our amazement when we discovered the trip was to an orphanage! The assignment was part of a humanitarian aid mission to Guinea Bissau, one of the poorest nations in the world. (Interestingly, though Philip was assigned more humanitarian aid trips, he never was assigned to an orphanage again.) Truly, the Lord accomplishes miracles. We ran into trials and frustrations as we navigated the adoption process through a third-world country, but to everyone's astonishment, little Peter and Abigail became ours within nine months, with visas issued less than twenty-four hours before our departure from Senegal.

So often, my strength to raise this family comes from the faith that Heavenly Father sets us up to succeed, not to fail. The chances of delivering two consecutive sets of twins are slim. The chances of completing a successful international adoption in less than a year without an intervening adoption agency are just as unlikely. Surely, these miracles came to be because the Lord desired them. Once I accepted that I was walking on the Lord's path, and not my own, He was free to accomplish miracles through me. The Lord tells us to "stand fast in the work wherewith I have called you" (D&C 9:14). We, the mothers of Zion, must be willing to hand over our lives to the Lord, walk a sometimes murky path, and He will indeed "lift us up" (D&C 9:14).

We will have stormy days. After all, motherhood is not without its challenges. It can be difficult, at times, to believe that your children are truly chosen spirits. When the little ones create murals on your freshly washed walls, or you race to a soccer game with preschoolers in tow to watch your little gem kick the ball into the wrong goal, you may wonder how "chosen" these kids really are. When you watch your teenager wasting precious time with the Xbox or demolishing the neighbor's garden with an awkward lurch of the car, you may continue to doubt. But there will be moments when you know. Maybe you will catch your child bearing his testimony to a younger sister or brother while doing chores or watch him volunteer a scripture at family devotional. There may be a moment when you groan because a child's light is on past bedtime, only to find that she is reading her scriptures. Illuminations like these will give you the strength to get out of bed another day, to drag yourself to the laundry room to sort the dirty clothes, or to start yet another meal.

Once the physical demands are met, we must deal with the intangible, but much more dangerous, issues. With a storm of secularism raging around us, and temptation lurking on every side, parents must watch carefully and judge wisely. What books should we check out of the library? What movies should we allow in the home? What limits will we place on technology? Will our children have cell phones, iPods, or an Xbox? How can we help a child choose a university? What kind of standards must the university maintain? What kind of clothes will we allow in this home, without being dowdy or unstylish? With whom will we foster friendships? How will we balance academics and extracurricular activities with service and Church obligations? I am constantly making decisions about the influences we have in our family. I have found that mothering calls on every aspect of my intellect and creativity.

The skills that I gained in the professional world

continue to be stretched. Multitasking, setting goals, and researching subjects to enrich my children (such as biotechnology, cultural history, and ceramics) keep me intellectually stimulated. I often use my organization skills to plan family field trips to places like the Metropolitan Art Museum, and research pieces of art ahead of time so that we will gain the most possible from the experience. The confidence I gained on stage as a pianist is a wonderful asset when exploring a foreign city in a fifteen-passenger van full of excited children. Poise has helped me deal with difficult situations, like shopping trips, where mothers of tidy broods of one or two look with horror as my children tear apart a store, searching for new Easter shoes. Marathon running in my younger days helped to prepare me for the daily race of motherhood. I am not the perfect mom, but the results of serious mothering show. I have confident, well-spoken children with ambitions and goals. They understand the importance of marriage and family. Most important, my children reflect the joy that sons and daughters of Heavenly Father should.

Mothering is a privilege. It is a divine calling. Our world, though it may deny it to the bitter end, needs righteous mothers desperately. Our children, these choice spirits of the latter days, need us to guide them, to love them, and to encourage them. Our world is still a beautiful place, if we can teach our children to look for the beauty. The "great and spacious building" is only too real, but so is the tree of life. Thrust yourself into your parenting responsibilities! As a mother of Zion, raise mothering to a higher standard. Use all your gifts—spiritual, intellectual, physical, and social—to give these children the foundation that they need to succeed.

Teach your daughters to be courageous and beautiful, strong and nurturing, intellectual and spiritual. Teach your sons to honor the priesthood, seek out knowledge, strengthen their bodies, and reach their goals. Teach your children that they are here for a unique reason, to follow a unique path. Teach them that they must walk hand in hand with the Lord each day to become the young men and women that He desires them to be. In the end, this is the mission that makes us tick. It's why we mothers do what we do.

# COMING HOME

*by Mindy Suttner*

There was a woman
Who had great talents and abilities.
But she also had an emptiness
In her heart.
So she set out to fill the void.

"I will change the world," she said.
"I will plant the earth."
And she did.
She planted flowers and ferns
And trees and grasses.
And the earth was beautiful.
But the emptiness deepened.

"I will write books," she said.
And she did.
She wrote of life and death
And the rise and fall of nations
And the light and dark in men's souls.
And man was enlightened.
But the emptiness persisted.

"I will lead nations," she said.
And she did.
She organized committees,
And collected food for the hungry,
And marched against social ills,
And ran for office,
And became president,
And led armies into battle,
And reduced the deficit,
And the economy surged.
But the emptiness ached within her.

Then one day,
During a brief reprieve
From the exhausting marathon
That was her life,
She took a moment to reflect
Upon her accomplishments.
And she heard a cry—
    A child sobbing.

She looked down to find a strange boy
Clinging to her knees.
She knelt to retrieve the child
And she realized that
It was her child.

And she saw the swollen eyes
And tearstained face and she realized
That he had been crying
For a very long time.

And she took the child
Into her arms
And held him
And comforted him.

Suddenly, she felt the sharp claws
Loosen their grip from around her heart.
And she thought,
"I will love my child."
And she did.

And the pain in her heart subsided.
And the void was filled.

And she wondered,
"Is it too late?"
But her child laughed.
And the rising sun
Draped the earth in lemon yellow
As she and her son
Skipped through the golden poppies
Of a new day.
And they were happy.
And the heavens rejoiced.

"I will change the world," she said.
And she did.

# ENDNOTES


1. M. Russell Ballard, "Daughters of God," *Ensign,* May 2008, 110.
2. Oxford Dictionaries Online, s.v. "fulfillment." http://oxforddictionaries.com/definition/fulfillment?region=us&q=fulfillment.
3. Gordon B. Hinckley, "Inspirational Thoughts," *Ensign*, March 2006, 3–4.
4. M. Russell Ballard, "Mothers and Daughters," *Ensign*, May 2010, 20.
5. Julie B. Beck, "Mothers Who Know," *Ensign*, Nov. 2007, 76–78.
6. David A. Bednar, "Pray Always," *Ensign,* Nov. 2008, 43.
7. James E. Faust, "A Message to My Granddaughters," *Ensign*, Sept. 1986, 20.
8. Spencer W. Kimball, *The Teachings of Spencer W. Kimball* (Salt Lake City: Bookcraft, 1995), 327; italics added.
9. David O. McKay, *Gospel Ideals: Selections from the Discourses of David O. McKay* (Salt Lake City: Improvement Era, 1953), 453–54.
10. Julie B. Beck, "Mothers Who Know," *Ensign*, Nov. 2007, 76–78.
11. L. Tom Perry, "Mothers Teaching Children in the Home," *Ensign*, May 2010, 31.
12. Harold B. Lee, *Teachings of the Presidents of the Church, Harold B. Lee*, "The Influence of Righteous Mothers" (Salt Lake City: The Church of Jesus Christ of Latter-day Saints, 2000), 139–40.
13. Joseph Smith, *Lectures on Faith* (Springville, UT: Cedar Fort, 2010), 3:5.
14. M. Russell Ballard, "Mothers and Daughters," *Ensign*, May 2010, 19.
15. Spencer W. Kimball, "Marriage is Honorable," *Speeches of the Year, 1973*, (Provo: Brigham Young University Press, 1974), 5.
16. Neal A. Maxwell, *Wherefore You Must Press Forward* (Salt Lake City: Deseret Book, 1977), 101.

# WORKS CITED


Ballard, M. Russell. "Daughters of God," *Ensign*, May 2008.

_______. "Mothers and Daughters," *Ensign*, May 2010.

Beck, Julie B. "Mothers Who Know," *Ensign*, November 2007.

Bednar, David A. "Pray Always," *Ensign*, Nov. 2008.

Faust, James E. "A Message to My Granddaughters," *Ensign*, September 1986.

Hinckley, Gordon B. "Inspirational Thoughts," *Ensign*, March 2006.

Kimball, Spencer W. *The Teachings of Spencer W. Kimball,* ed. Edward L. Kimball. Salt Lake City: Bookcraft, 1982.

______. "Marriage is Honorable," Speeches of the Year, 1973. Provo, Utah: Brigham Young University Press, 1973.

Lee, Harold B. *Teachings of the Presidents of the Church, Harold B. Lee*, "The Influence of Righteous Mothers." Salt Lake City: The Church of Jesus Christ of Latter-day Saints, Intellectual Reserve, 2000.

Maxwell, Neal A. *Wherefore Ye Must Press Forward.* Salt Lake City: Deseret Book, 1977.

McKay, David O. *Gospel Ideals: Selections from the Discourses of David O. McKay*. Salt Lake City: Improvement Era, 1953.

Oxford Dictionaries Online, s.v. "fulfillment." http://oxforddictionaries.com/definition/fulfillment?region=us&q=fulfillment.

Perry, L. Tom. "Mothers Teaching Children in the Home," *Ensign,* May 2010.

Smith, Joseph. *Lectures on Faith*. Springville, UT: Cedar Fort, 1985.

# CONTRIBUTORS AND EDITORS

**GEORGIA (YPMA) BONNEY** is the mother of fourteen children and a military wife. Formerly a lecturer and performer, she completed her piano performance degree and graduated magna cum laude from UCLA as a Regents Scholar, Alumni Scholar, and National Merit Scholar. After completing two master's degrees at the University of Southern California (in piano performance and collaborative piano), she attended the Vienna Conservatory in Austria as a Fulbright Scholar. During this time, she and her husband performed firesides in Croatia, Ukraine, Hungary, Serbia, and Slovenia. Philip and Georgia have also performed as part of the Temple Square series in Salt Lake City. Their family now lives near Vicenza, Italy.

**GRETCHEN (FUHRIMAN) CHENEY** is an Idaho girl, born and raised in Boise with her seven siblings. She graduated from Brigham Young University–Idaho with a bachelor of science in elementary education. While attending BYU–Idaho, Gretchen met and married her husband, Kirk Cheney. Gretchen welcomed her first child, Carter, in April 2008 while Kirk was attending Yale Law School. She was blessed with a daughter, Wendy, in July 2010. Gretchen now lives with her husband and children in Houston, Texas, where she is a full-time mother.

Raised in the Washington, DC metropolitan area, **SARAH (JENSEN) CLAYTON** earned a BA in history from Brigham Young University and a master's degree in education policy and management from Harvard University. Following graduate school, Sarah was named a Presidential Management Fellow and worked at both the White House and the US Department of Education. Since getting married, she has transitioned to the private sector and now works as a management consultant. Sarah served her mission in Milwaukee, Wisconsin, and currently lives in New York City with her husband and two children.

**LIA (SUTTNER) COLLINGS** grew up in St. George, Utah, the eldest of eight children. She studied classics and business at Brigham Young University, where she worked for three years as a researcher on the Joseph Smith Papers project. She and her family recently returned to Connecticut after a year in Berlin. She loves to read, exercise, make music, and bake bread. Some not-too-distant day, she hopes to return to classics and write the definitive study of ancient Greek education.

**LORI (RASMUSSEN) DAVIS** was raised in Albuquerque, New Mexico. She graduated from Brigham Young University in history with minors in music and linguistics. She then worked as an editor for LexisNexis and freelanced as a proofreader, writer, and musician. She currently lives in Munich, Germany, with her husband and two-year-old daughter.

**ROSALYN (COLLINGS) EVES** currently lives with her husband and three small children in southern Utah, where she teaches writing part time at the local university. She has a BA in English from BYU and an MA and PhD (also in English) from Penn State. She served a mission in Budapest, Hungary. In her spare time, she likes to read, write, try new recipes, watch movies with her husband (British period drama is her favorite), go for walks, and generally avoid anything that resembles housework.

**JENNIFER (GARDNER) FRAHM** grew up in Utah and Arizona, the second of seven children. Jennifer then moved to Connecticut, where she earned BA and MA degrees in European and Russian studies from Yale University, met and married her husband, Walker, and gave birth to their son, Atticus. She also spent time away from her studies serving a mission in Sweden. Jennifer currently lives in Seattle, where she runs a piano studio, teaches a community music class, volunteers at her local garden, and enjoys running and hiking. Atticus enthusiastically joins her in most of these pursuits.

**ELISE (BABBEL) HAHL** was raised in a loving family of ardent Phillies fans, just outside of Philadelphia. She studied English and economics at Stanford University, served a mission in Manaus, Brazil, and went on to earn a master's degree in writing (with an emphasis in nonfiction) from Johns Hopkins University. She lives with her husband and children in Belmont, Massachusetts, where she enjoys running, playing the piano, wrestling her three sons into submission, and working as a freelance writer and editor.

**KEELY (BAISDEN) KNUDSEN** is the mother of four (Saviah, Liviana, Wynter, and Emery) and wife to Brian W. Knudsen. She graduated first in her class with a BFA from New York University's Tisch School of the Arts and received a master's degree in drama on full scholarship from The Royal Scottish Academy of Music and Drama. A member of Actors' Equity Association, Keely has performed internationally in plays, musicals, operas, and dance companies and has choreographed and directed dozens of theatrical productions. Locally, she has been the director of education for the Elm Shakespeare Company and has taught at Yale University, Fairfield University, Hartt School of Drama, Southern Connecticut State University, and Quinnipiac University. Keely and her family reside in Guilford, Connecticut, where she is the founder and artistic director of the Legacy Theatre (www.LegacyTheatreCT.org).

**MARIANNE (WATTS) KRACZEK** was born and raised in the Washington, DC, area. She attended Utah State University and graduated in 1998 with a BS in political science and journalism. She served a mission in Spokane, Washington. After college graduation, she taught high school social studies and publications in Las Vegas, Nevada, and later worked as a graphic designer in New Haven, Connecticut, before her first child was born in 2003. She is currently a stay-at-home mother and lives in Orem, Utah, with her husband and three beautiful children.

**ADDIE (LYLE) LADUKE** earned a bachelors in design from Arizona State University with a minor in English. Before having children, she helped design several auto dealerships, golf clubhouses, and Elizabeth Arden Salons and still does some graphic design from her home. She lives in Chandler, Arizona, with her inspirational husband and three wonderful children. (Photo courtesy of Jessica Downey.)

**BECCA (FINDLAY) LLOYD** received her MA in art history from Brigham Young University and worked at Beinecke Rare Book and Manuscript Library at Yale University. Becca has presented her art history research at conferences in the United States and Europe. She is now a full-time mother in New Haven, Connecticut, where she lives with her husband and three young children.